THE
JAMES BOND
GIRLS

THE
JAMES BOND
GIRLS

GRAHAM RYE

BXTREE

For Mum and Dad — forever supportive

The author would like to express his thanks to:
John Cork, Lee Flint, Mollie Humphrey, Lee Pfeiffer, Lancelot Narayan, Andrew Pilkington, Alex Pow-Williams, and Dave Worrall. With special thanks to Tim Greaves.

The publishers would like to point out that the cast and credit lists for each film are selective and do not, in any case, represent full credit listings.

Many photographers covered the Bond sets over the years. To pay tribute, we mention the following few: Graham Attwood, John Bryson, Bert Cann, Albert Clarke, Frank Connor, Loomis Dean, Arthur Evans, Greg Gorman, Keith Hamshere, Ray Hearne, David Hurn, David James, Peter Kernot, Douglas Kirkland, Herman Leonard, Patrick Morin, Terry O'Neill, Joe Pearce, Bob Penn, George Rodger, Simon Wide, David Steen, James and Linda Swarbrick, and George Whitear.

The James Bond 007 International Fan Club & Archive, PO Box 007, Addlestone, Surrey KT15 1DY, England.
Email: jbifc@globalnet.co.uk
Url: http://www.thejamesbondfanclub.co.uk

Text first published in Great Britain 1989 by Boxtree Limited

This edition published 1999 by Boxtree an imprint of Macmillan Publishers Limited 25 Eccleston Place London SW1W 9NF
Basingstoke and Oxford

Associated companies throughout the world.

www.macmillan.co.uk

British Library Cataloguing in Publication Data
Rye, Graham
The James Bond Girls
Cinema Films, Characters, James Bond
Title
791.43'52
ISBN 0-7522-1147-1

Designed by DW Design, London
Printed in the U.K. by Bath Press, Glasgow

The James Bond Girls deals with the series of nineteen James Bond 007 films, from **Dr.No** to **The World Is Not Enough**, produced by Eon Productions Limited.
It does not include **Casino Royale** or **Never Say Never Again**, which were not made by Eon. Publication of this book has not been authorised by Eon Productions Limited.

Dr. No (1962)

JAMES BOND	SEAN CONNERY
HONEY RIDER	URSULA ANDRESS
DR. NO	JOSEPH WISEMAN
FELIX LEITER	JACK LORD
M	BERNARD LEE
MISS TARO	ZENA MARSHALL
SYLVIA	EUNICE GAYSON
MISS MONEYPENNY	LOIS MAXWELL
PRODUCERS	HARRY SALTZMAN*
	ALBERT R. BROCCOLI*
DIRECTOR	TERENCE YOUNG
SCREENPLAY	RICHARD MAIBAUM
	JOHANNA HARWOOD
	BERKLEY MATHER
DIRECTOR OF PHOTOGRAPHY	TED MOORE
PRODUCTION DESIGNER	KEN ADAM

*THE LISTING AS SHOWN IS CONTRACTUAL FOR THE EASTERN HEMISPHERE AND IS REVERSED FOR THE WESTERN HEMISPHERE.

THE EXOTIC Caribbean island of Jamaica, where Ian Fleming wrote his exciting spy novels, is the picturesque setting for *Dr. No*, the first James Bond film.

After indulging in verbal foreplay with Sylvia Trench at the gaming tables of his London club, James Bond reports to the offices of the British Secret Service. He learns from M that Strangways, their agent in Jamaica, has disappeared along with his secretary. Bond's mission is to investigate their disappearance and discover if it is linked with the 'toppling' of American missiles. Returning to his apartment, Bond is surprised to find Sylvia has gained entry. Dressed only in Bond's pyjama top and high-heeled shoes and practising her putting stroke, Sylvia is put off her aim when Bond bursts in, gun in hand. Her face is a picture of disappointment when Bond tells her he must leave immediately. After a kiss he relents – 'almost immediately', he tells her.

No sooner has he landed at Kingston airport than Bond finds that a beautiful female photographer attempts to take his picture and his chauffeur tries to kill him. Suddenly, the exotic island has taken on a more sinister appearance. Bond pays a return visit to Government House and, on leaving the governor's office, catches his secretary, Miss Taro, listening at

ABOVE: *(left) Sean Connery and Ursula Andress pose for publicity shots taken in Pinewood Studios' famed 'pool studio'.*
(right) Not a mango tree in sight! Ursula Andress brightens up the boat boys' day on location in Jamaica.

After the lovemaking she tells him she will cook dinner at home, in an attempt to keep him at the bungalow, but Bond will have none of it. He is feeling Italian and musical and orders a 'taxi' to take them to a restaurant. On its arrival Miss Taro is decidedly upset when she realizes the 'taxi' holds the local police. 'Book her, Superintendent, and mind her nail varnish,' says Bond as he pushes her into the car. She spits in Bond's face.

Bond places the pillows in Taro's bed to give the appearance of a sleeping man, retires to a chair, gun in hand, and waits. Some time later a hand appears from behind the bedroom door holding a silenced gun which fires six shots into the 'sleeping figure'. The hand belongs to Professor Dent, and Bond has him at a distinct disadvantage. Dent stalls for time while he clumsily tries to edge his fallen gun nearer. Dent lunges for his gun and fires at Bond, only to hear the hammer fall on an empty magazine. Bond points his Walther PPK menacingly at Dent: 'That's a Smith & Wesson, and you've had your six.' Bond shoots him dead.

the keyhole. Bond decides she bears closer investigation and suggests that she shows him around the island.

After preliminary investigations, Bond discovers the only person who claims to have seen Strangways's new secretary is the suspicious Professor Dent. After finding a receipt from Dent Laboratories at Strangways's bungalow, Bond questions the nervous Professor about the rock samples which the agent had brought to him. Dent says nothing that quells Bond's instinctive doubts about him, so Bond enlists the help of the local fisherman, Quarrel, and CIA agent, Felix Leiter. After checking Quarrel's boat with a Geiger counter, Bond discovers that the rock samples Strangways gathered were radioactive. Either Dent is a bad professor or a poor liar! Bond is determined to find out which.

That evening Bond drives to Miss Taro's bungalow in the mountains for a dinner date. En route he narrowly escapes death at the wheel of his car when a large black hearse attempts to run him off the mountain road. Unfortunately for the 'mourners', they are not so lucky and plummet over the cliff edge to an explosive death. Not surprisingly, Miss Taro is almost speechless at Bond's safe arrival. Telling her, 'I thought I was invited up here to admire the view', they retire to the bedroom.

ABOVE: (right) Sylvia Trench (Eunice Gayson) brings a whole new meaning to the word foreplay, surprising Bond (Sean Connery) in his Chelsea flat. Unfortunately agent 007 has instructions to leave for Jamaica immediately, but, seeing her grip of the game, he relents, leaving 'almost immediately'.

Arriving two hours late at Kingston harbour, Bond sets off into the night with Quarrel to investigate the island from which Strangways had collected the radioactive samples – the island of Crab Key, owned by the mysterious Dr. No. Landing safely on the island, the two men bed down for the night. Bond is woken from his sleep by the sound of a girl singing 'Underneath the Mango Tree'. He is treated to the sight of a bikini-clad Venus rising from the ocean. Bond's appearance from the undergrowth startles her. 'What are you doing here? Looking for shells?' she asks. 'No, I'm just looking,' he replies glibly. Bond learns that her name is Honey Rider and that she has been orphaned by Dr. No. She seems carefree and unafraid of discovery by the island's guards as she regularly frequents Crab Key. However, Bond knows it will be different this time.

Bond, Quarrel and Honey successfully evade Dr. No's guards in the mangrove swamps, but after battling with the island's 'dragon' – a diesel-engined swamp vehicle – Quarrel falls victim to its flame-throwing breath, while Bond and Honey are captured by guards wearing protective suits. Bond and Honey are taken to Dr. No's decontamination chamber, where they are scrubbed clean to reduce the dangerous radioactive levels their bodies have absorbed in the swamp. Sister Rose and Sister Lily minister to both Bond and Honey's every whim, although Bond's suggestion of two plane tickets to London is politely ignored. After recovering from drugged

coffee, Bond and Honey dress for dinner with their gracious host – Dr. No.

Bond and Honey take the elevator into No's underground lair, where they are astonished to see a huge glass observation panel with a perfect view of the undersea world. Bond's thoughts are interrupted when a voice from behind interjects, 'One million dollars, Mr Bond, you were wondering what it cost. The glass is convex, ten inches thick, which accounts for the magnifying effect.' Bond persistently tries to provoke Dr. No. 'Minnows pretending they're whales. Just like you on this island, Dr. No,' retorts Bond. 'It depends, Mr Bond, on which side of the glass you are,' counters No, winning on points. Over dinner Dr. No explains he works for SPECTRE – Special Executive for Counterintelligence Terrorism Revenge and Extortion. He admits that he thought there might even have been a place for Bond with SPECTRE. Bond tells him he would prefer the revenge department, but of course his first job would be to find the man who killed Strangways and Quarrel. Dr. No is not amused. Telling Bond he is 'just a stupid policeman', Dr. No leaves for his control room and orders his guards to soften up his dinner guest.

Bond regains consciousness on the bunk in a prison cell. After negotiating the electrified ventilator grille, he finds himself crawling through the air-conditioning system. Surviving an attempt to drown him in the tunnelling, Bond makes his way into Dr. No's control room disguised as a technician. During his attempt to destroy the nuclear reactor and abort Dr. No's sabotage of the American missile launch, Bond battles with Dr. No on the descending gantry overlooking the reactor's cooling tank. Bond gains the upper hand and Dr. No is submerged in the now boiling reactor tank when his metal hands are unable to grip the steel legs of the sinking gantry.

Racing from the deserted control room, Bond discovers Honey bound hand and foot with water rushing towards her from a sluice gate. Cutting her free, they escape in a small boat just before the reactor reaches critical mass, destroying Dr. No's complex in a shattering explosion. Drifting in their boat after running out of fuel, Bond and Honey are rescued by Felix Leiter and a detachment of marines. However, once taken in tow the castaways decide now is not the time to be rescued and release the tow line during an embrace.

AFTER THE runaway success of the first James Bond film this blueprint was adhered to, and is one of the contributing reasons for the longevity of the series.

It was planned that Eunice Gayson (real name Eunice Sargaison) would appear in successive Bond films as 007's home-grown romantic interest, Sylvia Trench, and eventually become Mrs Bond. However, she disappeared from the series after *From Russia With Love* (1963). Born in 1931, she trained for the opera, and entered films in 1948, with an appearance in

ABOVE: *Her nasty little habit of listening at keyholes arouses 007's suspicion that Miss Taro (Zena Marshall) is linked to the murder of Strangways and his secretary.*

My Brother Jonathan. Other roles followed with *Miss Robin Hood* (1952) and *The Revenge of Frankenstein* (1958). She also appeared in many British TV film series and was active in the theatre during the Seventies. She now lives quietly in Surrey, England. Her daughter, Kate, had a small role in *GoldenEye* (1995).

Miss Taro, Dr. No's pawn in the game of kiss 'n' kill, as portrayed by Zena Marshall, was another role in a long line of bad girls and conniving women. She could often be seen in Edgar Wallace thrillers on the arm of a criminal or crooked businessman. Born in Kenya in 1925, she made her stage debut in repertory and her first film was *Caesar and Cleopatra* (1945). She also appeared in *The Embezzler* (1954), *The Scarlet Web* (1954), *Those Magnificent Men in their Flying Machines* (1965) and *The Terrornauts* (1967). Now retired, she divides her time between London and the South of France.

ABOVE: *(top) 'Mind her nail varnish!' Bond (Sean Connery) kills time with Miss Taro (Zena Marshall) before handing her over to the Kingston police. (bottom) Margaret LeWars's 'freelance' photographer attempts to capture Bond on film when he arrives at Kingston Airport, and later at Pussfeller's nightclub. (right) Honey (Ursula Andress) in the bikini that launched a million sighs from red-blooded males in audiences around the world.*

Undoubtedly the most memorable of all the Bond girls is Ursula Andress as Honey Rider. The sequence in which she rises from the sea was to secure her screen immortality, and was an image by which all subsequent Bond girls would be judged. Born in March 1939 in Berne, Switzerland, Ursula was the daughter of a Swiss diplomat, and showed unusual aptitude in art and chemistry at the Neue Mädchen Schule in Berne. After appearing in many school theatrical productions she was determined to make a career in show business. She found herself in Hollywood at eighteen, where Marlon Brando encouraged her to try acting. Her screen debut came in *The Loves of Casanova* (1962) and subsequent minor roles followed. It was not until her exposure in *Dr. No* (1962) that her face became internationally known. Her best known appearances include *Fun in Acapulco* (1964) with Elvis Presley, *She* (1965), *What's New Pussycat?* (1965), the James Bond spoof *Casino Royale* (1967), *Red Sun* (1971), directed by Terence Young, and *Clash of the Titans* (1981). Her private life always seemed to overshadow her career, and she was much in the news when she became a mother at 44 in 1980. She has now generally retired from acting.

ABOVE & OPPOSITE: *Honey with a bunny! The publicity photographers used Ursula Andress's stunning figure to full advantage to promote* Dr. No.
The nude portfolio she posed for in Playboy *is now, not suprisingly, a much-sought-after collector's item.*

From Russia With Love (1963)

JAMES BOND	SEAN CONNERY
TATIANA ROMANOVA	DANIELA BIANCHI
KERIM BEY	PEDRO ARMENDARIZ
ROSA KLEBB	LOTTE LENYA
RED GRANT	ROBERT SHAW
M	BERNARD LEE
MISS MONEYPENNY	LOIS MAXWELL
MAJOR BOOTHROYD (Q)	DESMOND LLEWELYN
PRODUCERS	HARRY SALTZMAN
	ALBERT R. BROCCOLI
DIRECTOR	TERENCE YOUNG
SCREENPLAY	RICHARD MAIBAUM
	JOHANNA HARWOOD
DIRECTOR OF PHOTOGRAPHY	TED MOORE
ART DIRECTOR	SYD CAIN

*F*rom Russia With Love has James Bond fighting for his life against the machinations of SPECTRE in its attempt to discredit the British Secret Service and gain personal revenge for the death of their operative Dr. No.

After receiving a letter from Tatiana Romanova, a cipher clerk at the Russian consulate in Istanbul, M – head of British Intelligence – summons agent James Bond to his office. The girl wants to defect, and as surety she claims she will bring with her the Lektor, a top-secret decoding device, but on one condition – that Bond is sent to bring her and the machine back to England. It appears she has fallen in love with the file photo of the British agent. Both Bond and M realize this is a trap, but if there is any chance of them getting a Lektor they really must look into it. Before Bond leaves, he is issued with a special black attaché case from Q branch. Major Boothroyd explains to 007 that if he opens the case incorrectly a tear gas cartridge hidden in a magnetized tin of talcum powder will explode – in his face. The case also contains a hidden throwing knife, an AR7 folding sniper's rifle and 50 gold sovereigns – 25 are secreted in each hinge strap. Bond describes this smart-looking piece of luggage as 'a nasty little Christmas present' and doubts he will need it on this mission. It is a rare occasion when agent 007 is proved to be very wrong.

Landing in Istanbul, Bond is driven from the airport to meet Kerim Bey – head of station T Turkey. He is followed by a mysterious black Citroën driven by Russian agents. Kerim tells Bond they must wait for the girl to arrange a meeting. He is followed once more on the journey to his hotel, but the car is now driven by SPECTRE assassin Red Grant. Bond checks into the hotel, only to discover that his room is bugged. Complaining that the bed is too small, he is given the only room left – the bridal suite. Meanwhile, Grant has left the Russian agent's car parked in front of their consulate – the driver dead on the back seat. The cold war in Istanbul will not remain cold very much longer.

ABOVE: *(left) Tatiana (Daniela Bianchi) has a bad hair day at the office when 007 takes the Lektor decoding machine from the Russian Consulate.*
(top) While visiting a gypsy camp Bond is thoroughly entertained by the undulating stomach muscles of a belly dancer (Leila Guiraut).
Leila, a professional belly dancer, also appeared in Days of Wine and Roses *(1962).*
OPPOSITE: *Aliza Gur poses with Sean Connery for a photo session which was used extensively in the US poster campaign.*

Kerim is 'relaxing' with his girlfriend when a limpet-mine attached to the wall outside explodes, devastating his office. The explosion was timed to catch him at his desk, and he cannot understand why his 'Russian friends' have broken the truce. In an effort to learn the reason behind the attack, Kerim and Bond spy on the consulate from an underground reservoir where Kerim has had a periscope secretly installed. Looking through the eyepiece, they discover the perpetrator of the bomb attack was a Bulgarian named Krilencu, whom the Russians use as a killer. 'You should remember him,' says Kerim. 'This man kills for pleasure.'

That evening Kerim takes Bond to an encampment of

attacker. The Bulgars are beaten off by superior force and Krilencu retreats. Kerim discovers the attack was yet another attempt on his life and he decides to pay Krilencu a final visit with Bond. Kerim and Bond wait in the street outside the killer's hideout. Finally, he is forced to leave through his secret escape exit – a door behind the girl's mouth on a gigantic movie billboard. As Krilencu climbs from his hideout, Kerim shoots him with Bond's sniper's rifle and he crashes to the pavement, dead. 'That pays many debts,' sighs Kerim. 'She should have kept her mouth shut!' suggests Bond.

Bond returns to his hotel exhausted, but soon perks up when he finds Tatiana in his bed wearing nothing but a black

gypsies, whose 'talents' he uses in a similar fashion to the way the Russians use the Bulgars. Unbeknown to Bond, Kerim and the gypsies, Krilencu and his men are already surrounding the camp. And also lurking in the shadows is Grant. Bond and Kerim have arrived on a bad night. There is to be a fight to the death between Vida and Zora, two gypsy girls who are rivals for the hand in marriage of the chief's son. The girls are led from their caravans and the fight commences. Bond watches, grim-faced, as the girls attack each other mercilessly. However, the fight is cut short when shots ring out. Krilencu and his men swarm into the camp, shooting at anything that moves. In the foray that follows, Kerim's gun jams and he is injured, and Bond is saved from certain death when Grant shoots an unseen

choker. 'Guns upset me,' says Tatiana, pushing Bond's Walther aside. 'Sorry, I'm a little upset myself,' says Bond. He hopes he will come up to Tatiana's expectations. 'I will tell you – in the morning,' she promises. Neither Bond nor Tania, as she is known to her friends, know that their bedroom antics are being filmed from behind a large mirror overseen by Rosa Klebb.

After checking the authenticity of the Lektor with Tania, Bond and Kerim devise a plan to steal the decoding machine from the consulate. Exploding a smoke bomb underneath the consulate as a diversion, Bond successfully steals the Lektor and escapes with Tania and Kerim, to board the Orient Express for the Bulgarian frontier and safety. They are spotted by Russian security man Benz, who leaps aboard as the train moves off. As

ABOVE: *(left) 'Back to the salt mines!' Kerim Bey, Head of Station T Turkey, is 'coaxed' back to the sofa by his sultry girlfriend (Nadja Regin).*
(right) Gypsy girls Zora (Martine Beswick) and Vida (Aliza Gur) are to fight to the death for the hand in marriage of the chief's son.
After the fight has been interrupted, Bond is 'given' the girls and left with the onerous task of deciding which one should marry the chief's son.
A dirty job – but someone's got to do it!

it leaves the station it is apparent that Grant is also on board. Leaving Kerim with Benz, Bond retires to his compartment to get some sleep. Later, Bond and Tania are about to leave for the restaurant car when the conductor announces, 'There's been a terrible accident!' Both Kerim and Benz are dead in their compartment. Apparently they have killed each other. Hurt and angry at the death of his friend, Bond tries to force Tania to tell him her orders. She says she cannot tell him: 'Even if you kill me, I cannot tell you.' Exasperated, Bond knocks her to the floor. At Belgrade he leaves the train to inform Kerim's son of his father's death, and tells him to arrange via M for someone to meet the train at Zagreb.

Grant intercepts his contact from M at Zagreb and kills him, then re-boards the train posing as the murdered Captain Nash and introduces himself to Bond. When Bond tells Grant he cannot risk taking the Lektor through customs, Grant shows him his planned escape route on a map. As Bond studies the route Grant knocks him unconscious and takes his gun. When Bond has regained his senses, Grant explains how SPECTRE planned to play the British off against the Russians and Bond realizes it was not the Russians' show after all.

Bond opens his briefcase to show Grant it contains gold sovereigns, with which he hopes to bargain for his life, and offers to open Nash's case, which should contain more. Bond's haste makes Grant suspicious and he decides to open it himself.

ABOVE: (left) Red Grant (Robert Shaw) has those everyday psychopathic stresses and strains eased away by a SPECTRE masseuse (Jan Williams).
(right) Taken at the same poster-art session (see page 13), Daniela Bianchi poses with Sean Connery. When the art director on the shoot arrived at photographer David Hurn's studio, he realized he had forgotten to bring Bond's gun. Luckily the photographer had a Walther LP53 .177 air pistol at his studio, for keeping the rat population in check. It was intended that the gun would eventually be retouched to resemble 007's PPK but this never happened.

As he does, the tear gas cartridge explodes in his face. Bond takes his chance and a vicious fight ensues. Grant almost overpowers Bond, but 007 takes a knife from the attaché case, and plunges it into Grant's arm before strangling him with the wire garrotte from his own wrist watch.

Bond and Tania leave the train, taking the truck that was part of Grant's escape route. They head for a bay where a speedboat is waiting, but en route they are attacked from the air by a SPECTRE helicopter. Bond shoots the co-pilot, who then drops a hand grenade inside the cockpit – with explosive results. Thinking they are safe at last, they head for Venice in their speedboat, only to be intercepted by a fleet of SPECTRE gunboats. However, Bond jettisons ruptured fuel drums, igniting them with two well-aimed flares. The SPECTRE fleet is engulfed in flames as Bond quips, 'There's a saying in England – where there's smoke there's fire!'

Now safely in their Venice hotel room, James Bond is making travel arrangements on the telephone when he sees the hotel maid pointing a gun at him. Too late, he realizes it is Klebb. Klebb is about to pull the trigger when Tania runs back into the room, knocking the gun from Klebb's hand. Panic-stricken, Klebb lashes out at Bond, attempting to kick him with the poisoned blade protruding from the tip of her shoe. As Bond defends himself with a chair Tania shoots Klebb with her own gun. The 'horrible woman' slides down the wall, dead. 'She's had her kicks,' Bond says glibly as he takes the gun from Tania's hand. Relaxing in a gondola with Tania, Bond remembers he still has the reel of film that was shot in the bridal suite. Tania asks him what it is. He tells her, 'I'll show you!'

IN THE series of James Bond movies, *From Russia With Love* is the most faithful to an Ian Fleming novel. Tatiana Romanova is yet another pawn in the villain's master plan.

Runner-up in the 1960 Miss Universe contest and a former Rome fashion model, Daniela Bianchi is a native Italian and after Bond went on to more obscure films like *Weekend Italian Style* (1965), *Dirty Heroes* (1967) and *Operation Kid Brother* (1967) with Sean Connery's brother Neil. She married a Genoan shipping magnate in 1970 by whom she has a son, Fillippo.

Whilst fighting gypsy girl Vida was portrayed by ex-Miss Israel Aliza Gur, her opponent was ex-Miss Jamaica Martine Beswick. Martine, still fabulous-looking in her sixties, first travelled to England at the age of 12 and completed her grammar school education at 16. She later entered Pitman's College, but left after one term to pursue a career in fashion modelling. In 1960 Martine's family returned to Jamaica. She got a job as an air hostess and did whatever freelance modelling she could. In 1961 she won the title of Miss Jamaica and used the prize money to return to England. She enrolled on a fashion modelling course and was soon working regularly for top publications. Her first contact with the Bond films was when her agent submitted her photos to the producers for the role of the Chinese girl in *Dr. No*. After an interview, it was decided her lack of experience outweighed her good looks, but she was promised a future role if she studied drama. A year later she was given her first dramatic role in *From Russia With Love*. Other roles followed in *The Amorous Adventures of Moll Flanders* (1965) and *The Sandpiper* (1965), before appearing with Bond again in *Thunderball* (1965).

ABOVE: *Kerim Bey's girlfriend. The sultry Nadja Regin was the first actress to appear in the 007 series twice in a different role.*
OPPOSITE: *Ex-Miss Rome Daniela Bianchi was picked from dozens of aspiring hopefuls for the role of Tatiana Romanova. Among them was top model Tania Mallet, who lost out because her voice was considered too upper-class English – an ironic decision in hindsight, as Bianchi was revoiced by British actress Barbara Jefford.*

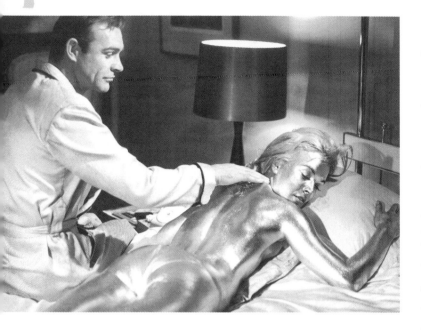

Goldfinger (1964)

JAMES BOND	SEAN CONNERY
PUSSY GALORE	HONOR BLACKMAN
GOLDFINGER	GERT FROBE
JILL MASTERSON	SHIRLEY EATON
TILLY MASTERSON	TANIA MALLET
ODDJOB	HAROLD SAKATA
M	BERNARD LEE
FELIX LEITER	CEC LINDER
MISS MONEYPENNY	LOIS MAXWELL
Q	DESMOND LLEWELYN
PRODUCERS	HARRY SALTZMAN
	ALBERT R. BROCCOLI
DIRECTOR	GUY HAMILTON
SCREENPLAY	RICHARD MAIBAUM
	PAUL DEHN
PRODUCTION DESIGNER	KEN ADAM
DIRECTOR OF PHOTOGRAPHY	TED MOORE

JAMES BOND is pitted against one of his most lethal adversaries, when Auric Goldfinger attempts to break into the world's largest gold depository – Fort Knox.

After escaping the wiles of Latin dancer Bonita and despatching drug smuggler Capungo to a shocking death, James Bond is relaxing at the poolside of the Miami Beach Hotel with Dink, a striking blonde.

Bond is observing the card playing antics of Auric Goldfinger, whom he suspects is a cheat. Entering Goldfinger's hotel room, Bond discovers blonde beauty Jill Masterson reclining on the balcony observing Goldfinger's card game through binoculars. By means of a receiver in Goldfinger's hearing-aid, she is transmitting the details of his opponent's hand. Bond warns Goldfinger that the Miami Beach police would not take kindly to what he is doing and tells him to start losing. $15,000 seems a generous amount, says Bond, and Goldfinger's face contorts in rage as he snaps his pencil in two. That evening Bond entertains Jill in his hotel bedroom, but while taking a fresh bottle of champagne from the fridge he is knocked unconscious from behind. Gathering his wits, he is shocked to find Jill is covered from head to toe in gold paint. She has died from skin suffocation. Goldfinger has exacted a terrible revenge.

After receiving a dressing-down from M for borrowing Goldfinger's girlfriend, and armed with a bar of gold recovered from a Nazi hoard in Lake Toplitz, Bond arranges an encounter with Goldfinger on the golf course. Goldfinger is neither surprised nor concerned when he meets Bond, although, after losing the match to him, he makes it quite clear that further intervention in his affairs would be unwise for 007's health. Goldfinger's Korean manservant Oddjob promptly throws his steel-rimmed bowler hat at a nearby statue, severing its head neatly. Bond comments, 'Remarkable, but what will the Club secretary have to say?' 'Oh, nothing, Mr Bond,' says Goldfinger, 'I own the Club.'

Following Goldfinger to Switzerland, Bond encounters a desperate girl in the form of Tilly Soames, but her luggage is initialled T.M. That night Bond stakes out Goldfinger's factory complex. Hearing someone creeping through the undergrowth, he discovers it to be Tilly. After Bond wrestles her to the ground she explains that she is Jill Masterson's sister and is determined to avenge her sister's death. Her rifle sets off a trip alarm and Goldfinger's Korean guards, led by Oddjob, are soon on the scene. Tilly runs for the trees as Bond opens fire on the guards from the cover of his Aston Martin DB5. There is a swishing sound followed by a sickening crack as Oddjob's bowler makes contact with Tilly's neck. Bond runs to her fallen body, but it is too late, she is dead. Captured, and with a guard in his car, Bond uses the passenger ejector seat at the first opportunity, and the guard flies out of the car roof. There follows a car chase around Goldfinger's factory, and Bond crashes into a brick wall and falls from the car. As Bond regains consciousness he realizes

ABOVE: *'All that glitters is not gold!' Bond (Sean Connery) discovers the gilded corpse of Jill Masterson (Shirley Eaton) in his Miami Beach Hotel bed.*
OPPOSITE: *(left) Cabaret dancer Bonita (Nadja Regin) is the bait in the honey trap to kill agent 007. (right) Shirley Eaton played one of two sisters who would both meet untimely deaths at the hands of Oddjob, Goldfinger's murderous manservant.*

that he is strapped to a table and Goldfinger is standing over him gloating in triumph as he gives a signal to the control room. The contraption in front of Bond starts to glow and move closer. Goldfinger explains it is an industrial laser which can project a spot on the moon, or at closer range cut through solid metal. He is determined to give Bond a demonstration. The laser beam begins to cut through the gold surface of the table, inching ever closer to Bond's groin. Bond admits that Goldfinger has made his point and thanks him for the demonstration. 'Choose your next witticism carefully, Mr Bond, it may be your last,' bellows Goldfinger. Bond is desperate. 'Do you expect me to talk?' 'No, Mr Bond, I expect

you to die!' comes the final word from Goldfinger. Only when Bond mentions 'Operation Grand Slam' does he relent to the worried insistence of his Chinese guest, Mr Ling, who has supplied him with the cobalt and iodine device which is to bring a cataclysmic conclusion to Goldfinger's masterplan. Bond is shot with a tranquillizer gun and soon loses consciousness again.

When Bond awakens he is sitting in an aeroplane with a beautiful woman pointing a gun at him. He is not dreaming, the woman is Goldfinger's personal pilot, Pussy Galore. They land and Bond is taken to 'Auric Stud', where he is held prisoner. Here he learns the full extent of Goldfinger's plans while hiding under a model of Fort Knox. Goldfinger plans to explode an atomic device in the heart of America's gold reserve, making it radioactive for 58 years, thereby increasing the value of his own supply ten times over. Pussy substitutes the deadly

nerve gas her pilots are to use in Goldfinger's plan. And Bond is handcuffed to the atomic device and left in the vaults of the Fort Knox bullion depository to die. Meanwhile, outside Fort Knox the 'gassed' American soldiers battle with Goldfinger's Korean troops. Seeing the day is lost, Goldfinger escapes, but inside the vault Oddjob battles Bond in a fight to the death. Bond is nearly vanquished by Oddjob's incredible strength, but electrocutes the giant Korean when he tries to retrieve his bowler hat which has become jammed between the bars of the vault room. Bond tries to stop the countdown on the bomb but to no avail. Felix Leiter arrives with a scientist who flicks the right switch in the very nick of time.

His mission accomplished, Bond boards an army plane to visit the President for a personal thank you for saving America's gold reserve, but, Goldfinger has taken over the plane. Bond warns him that it is dangerous to fire guns in aircraft and, distracting his attention, lunges for his gun. The two men wrestle for its possession. The gun goes off, shattering a window, and as the cabin depressurizes Goldfinger is sucked through the broken window. Bond struggles to the cabin, where Pussy is fighting to gain control of the aircraft. 'Where's Goldfinger?' she asks. 'Playing his golden harp,' quips Bond.

ABOVE: *Golden girls are forever! Shirley Eaton's three minutes of screen time in* Goldfinger *eclipsed the rest of her substantial career in the public's mind.*

roles followed in *Around the World Under the Sea* (1965), *The Scorpio Letters* (1966) and *The Seven Men of Sumuru* (1969).

Tania Mallet abandoned modelling to co-star in *Goldfinger* as Tilly Masterson. She didn't take to acting and subsequent offers were met with a blank refusal. She married twice, inheriting three step children with her second husband, a toy manufacturer. She enjoys gardening. *Goldfinger* was her only screen role.

Born in 1925, Honor Blackman's wartime career as a Home Office despatch rider seemed to brand her as the adventurous type but, having enrolled in the Rank Charm School, it was decided to cast her as an English Rose. It was not until many years later that she was able to break her screen image with the portrayal of Pussy Galore. 'Before Bond, the parts I used to play in films were demure, sweet, antiseptic and antisex,' she said. 'I wasn't even allowed to think like a woman. Pussy Galore and 007 worked wonders for me.' It was unnecessary for her to test for the role as the film-makers already knew what she could do from her appearances in TV's *The Avengers*. At the time of the film's release, there was an uproar over the name Pussy Galore and the film-makers were unable to get it past the American censors. Then *Goldfinger*

The couple parachute to safety, and when a rescue helicopter hovers by, Bond pulls Pussy under the 'chute telling her, 'Oh no you don't, this is no time to be rescued!'

THE WOMEN in *Goldfinger* are mainly victims, although Pussy Galore was a reflection of the more liberated and self-sufficient women of the Sixties.

'This kind of exposure is marvellous for my career,' said Shirley Eaton of her role as Jill Masterson in *Goldfinger*. Shirley's gold-painted body is probably one of the most enduring images of any Bond film. It even graced the cover of LIFE magazine. The gilding of Shirley had to be done to a strict time limit set by the studio doctors. They warned that after 60 minutes, the continued blocking of the pores by the paint could be dangerous. When the studio make-up man slapped the paint on her 36-22-36 figure, with a doctor and nurse standing by, Shirley gurgled happily. 'It tickles,' she giggled as the brush covered her neck, her back, and even the soles of her feet. A six-inch square on her midriff was left clear of paint as an added precaution – on a doctor's insistence. 'I had flu at the time and it was very uncomfortable – but I felt like a real golden gal,' said Shirley. Her appearance in *Goldfinger* only lasted three minutes, but it is a role that everyone always remembers. After the death of her husband she returned to the UK from the South of France, where they lived together for many years. She abandoned acting in 1969 to devote herself to her family but in more recent years has been trying to make a comeback. Born in 1936, her first film appearance was *You Know What Sailors Are* (1954), and other

ABOVE: *(top) Photographed at Stoke Poges Golf Club, model turned actress, Tania Mallet brought a haughty Englishness to the role of Tilly Masterson. (bottom) 'Make hay not war!' Honor Blackman shares a few falls with Bob Simmons – Sean Connery's stunt double, and stunt arranger on the Bond series from* Dr.No *to* Octopussy.

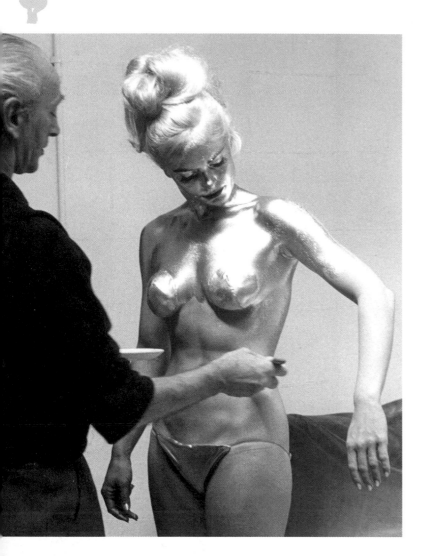

opened in London and Honor was presented to Prince Philip. The next day the newspapers ran a picture of them headlined 'Pussy and the Prince'. That was the clincher. The American censor gave the film the all-clear. Honor's career has been consistently successful on stage, screen and TV, notably during the Nineties in *The Upper Hand*. Other films include *Jason and the Argonauts* (1963), *A Twist of Sand* (1967), *Shalako* (1968) with Sean Connery, and *The Cat and the Canary* (1976).

Two of the smaller roles in *Goldfinger* warrant mention. Nadja Regin, the Latin nightclub dancer Bonita, is one of the few actresses who hold the distinction of appearing in two Bond movies, her other being *From Russia With Love* (1963), in which she played Kerim Bey's girlfriend; while Margaret Nolan as Dink shared a poolside scene with Sean Connery and is also the 'golden girl' featured in Robert Brownjohn's opening and closing credit titles for *Goldfinger*.

ABOVE: *(top left) Shirley Eaton undergoes a second gilding for the Pinewood photo shoot which appeared in LIFE magazine.*
(top right) 1 August 1964: 007 is menaced by the Masterson sisters and Pussy Galore in this wonderfully over the top publicity shot, taken on Ken Adam's fabulous Fort Knox set at Pinewood Studios.
(bottom) Publicity shot of Nadja Regin who portrayed Bonita. With a figure like this, how did 007 ever see the reflection of his assailant in her eyes?

ABOVE: *(top) James Bond's stunning 'haymate' – Honor Blackman as Pussy Galore. (middle & right) Glamour model Margaret Nolan (also known as Vickie Kennedy) featured in the movie as Dink, and also in the stunning credit titles. (left) On the Miami Beach Hotel set, Sean Connery chats with Shirley Eaton, and 007's creator, Ian Fleming.*

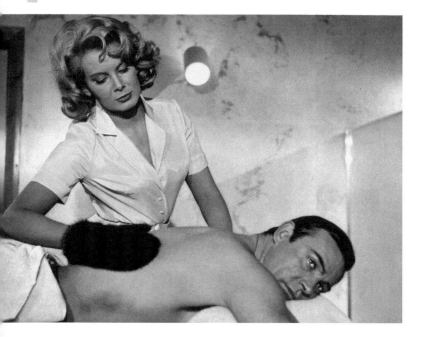

Thunderball (1965)

JAMES BOND	SEAN CONNERY
DOMINO	CLAUDINE AUGER
LARGO	ADOLFO CELI
FIONA	LUCIANA PALUZZI
FELIX LEITER	RIK VAN NUTTER
M	BERNARD LEE
MISS MONEYPENNY	LOIS MAXWELL
Q	DESMOND LLEWELYN
PRESENTED BY	HARRY SALTZMAN
	ALBERT R. BROCCOLI
PRODUCER	KEVIN McCLORY
DIRECTOR	TERENCE YOUNG
SCREENPLAY	RICHARD MAIBAUM
	JOHN HOPKINS
BASED ON THE ORIGINAL STORY BY	KEVIN McCLORY,
	JACK WHITTINGHAM AND
	IAN FLEMING
PRODUCTION DESIGNER	KEN ADAM
DIRECTOR OF PHOTOGRAPHY	TED MOORE

Thunderball takes James Bond to the Bahamas in search of a hijacked Vulcan bomber and its deadly cargo of nuclear bombs stolen by the criminal organization SPECTRE.

After despatching an old enemy in France with the aid of Sûreté agent Mademoiselle La Porte, Bond takes a rest cure at the health farm Shrublands. Here he becomes involved with his physiotherapist, Patricia Fearing, and survives an attempt on his life by SPECTRE agent Count Lippe. On leaving the health farm in his specially equipped Aston Martin DB5, Bond is followed by Lippe, who opens fire on him with a revolver.

ABOVE: *(left) 'Mink - it soothes the tension!' In a scene cut from the final film, Bond (Sean Connery) is given a relaxing rub down with a mink glove by 'physical' therapist Patricia (Molly Peters). (right) Later, Bond returns the favour in his bedroom at Shrublands Health Farm. (Bottom) 'Two's company, three's the director'. Much to their amusement, Terence Young joins Molly Peters and Sean Connery for a tea break.*

Before Bond is able to use the Aston's special armaments, a speeding motorbike fires two deadly rockets at Lippe's car, sending it crashing off the road, where it explodes in a ball of flame. Bond is to meet the motorcyclist later – but in very different circumstances.

When Bond reports to M that he has seen the pilot of the missing Vulcan bomber dead at the health farm it prompts the Secret Service chief to assign him to Nassau, where the pilot's sister, Domino, is living. Bond arrives in the Bahamas and teams up with the Service's local agent, Paula Catlin, and CIA agent Felix Leiter. Bond makes initial contact with Domino when he admires her form underwater. Later, when he meets her at the casino, he learns she is the mistress of Emilio Largo, whose yacht, the *Disco Volante,* is suspected of carrying the stolen atom bombs. The following night Bond inspects the hull of the *Disco Volante* underwater and is attacked by a frogman sentry. The alarm is raised and Bond is pursued by Largo's men, who proceed to throw grenades into the water in order to depth-charge the unknown intruder. Faking his death, Bond eludes Largo's men and swims to shore. A speeding car stops to give him a lift. The driver is SPECTRE agent Fiona Volpe – the motorcyclist who despatched Lippe in England. Bond notices she is wearing a large ring identical to one worn by Largo. Coincidentally, Fiona happens to be staying at the same hotel as Bond.

Bond investigates Largo's home, Palmyra, when Leiter reports that Paula is missing. Bond discovers her dead by her own hand in the basement of Largo's island headquarters. She has taken cyanide rather than suffer at the hands of her captors.

Bond barely escapes with his life when he has an exceedingly close encounter in the shark pool. Once back at his

ABOVE: *(left) Martine Beswick poses in one of the many startling swimsuits used for publicity shots – but unfortunately, never seen in the movie. (right) The impressively elegant Claudine Auger looks equally eye-stopping whether trimmed in fur or . . .*

hotel, Bond discovers Fiona has now been moved into Paula's room. When Bond finds Fiona in the bath she asks him to hand her something to put on. Bond, ever the gentleman, hands her her slippers! They retire to the bedroom, and after the lovemaking, Fiona shows her true colours when Bond is taken prisoner by Largo's henchmen – but not before Fiona has made her feelings about Bond quite clear. 'James Bond, who only has to make love to a woman and she starts to hear heavenly choirs singing. She repents and immediately returns to the side of right and virtue – but not this one! What a blow it must have been, *you* having a failure.' Bond's comment – 'Well, you can't win them all!'

Bond escapes from his captors and is chased through the Junkanoo carnival. Fiona catches up with him at the Kiss Kiss Club, where on the dance floor she steers him towards the

waiting gun of her henchman. At the last moment Bond spins round, and the bullet meant for him hits Fiona in the back and kills her instantly. Bond leaves her body seated at one of the club tables, asking a couple dining, 'Do you mind if my friend sits this one out – she's just dead!'

Bond and Domino visit Love Beach, where he tells her of the death of her brother. Domino asks Bond to promise that he will kill Largo for her. Their conversation is overheard by Vargas, Largo's henchman, who has followed them. Domino warns Bond as Vargas levels his pistol ready for the kill. Bond turns unexpectedly, firing his spear-gun, which pins Vargas to a palmtree – 'I think he got the point!'

After escaping from an underwater cavern where he had been stranded by Largo, Bond leads the American aqua-troopers against the SPECTRE chief and his force of frogmen in a fierce and bloody underwater battle. Largo escapes aboard

ABOVE: *(left) ... wearing a bikini designed to reflect her character's name – Domino. (right) In her screen test, Molly Peters was still a natural brunette. At the last moment it was decided that the women involved with Bond should all have different hair colouring, so Molly became a blonde.*
OPPOSITE: *This photograph amply illustrates why Molly's character in* Thunderball *was known as a 'physical therapist'.*

thought her 37-24-37 figure would secure her future as a glamour model, and taking their advice she became a pin-up and nude photo-model. It was while she was one of a crowd of extras in a scene for *The Amorous Adventures of Moll Flanders* (1965) that she was spotted by the film's director, Terence Young. After she had appeared in her second film, *Joey Boy* (1965), Young, the director of *Thunderball*, suggested that she audition for the role of Patricia. Molly was the first nude – albeit in silhouette behind

the *Disco Volante* as his men are overcome by the superior American forces, aided by Bond wearing his underwater jet-pack. Climbing aboard the speeding hydrofoil Bond battles with Largo and his cabin crew. He is knocked senseless to the floor, and Largo is about to shoot him when Domino appears from below deck and fires a harpoon in the SPECTRE chief's back. Largo slumps dead over the hydrofoil's controls. 'I'm glad he's dead,' says Domino. 'You're glad!' retorts Bond. Realizing the SPECTRE chief has jammed the controls of the hydrofoil, Bond and Domino leap into the relative safety of the sea as the *Disco Volante* runs aground on the rocks, exploding on impact. Sitting in a rubber dinghy, a puzzled Domino watches as Bond inflates a large red balloon tied to a rope which he clips to his diving suit. The balloon floats into the air, where an American Air Force plane catches the rope and whisks Bond and Domino into the air – and safety.

THE WOMEN in *Thunderball* are more assertive than those in the previous three films, although Bond is still allowed the obligatory 'plaything'.

Molly Peters, who portrayed the 'physical' therapist Patricia Fearing, hails from Walsham-le-Willows in Suffolk, England, and was a brunette prior to her role in *Thunderball*. She left her parents' farm in 1960 to come to London, where she started work as a shop girl. Many of Molly's London friends

frosted glass – to appear in a Bond film. She has now retired from acting and lives with her husband in Suffolk.

Fiona Volpe, the redheaded SPECTRE killer, was one of the most memorable female roles in the entire series. This girl meant to kill Bond – and anyone else who stood in her way! Portrayed by Italian actress Luciana Paluzzi, this was a bad girl who enjoyed being bad! Among her many film and TV roles Luciana also appeared in *The Man from U.N.C.L.E.* film *To Trap a Spy* (1965), in which she also tried to kill Napoleon Solo. She has also appeared in *Chuka* (1967), *The Amazons* (1973) and *The Cop That Loves Me* (1978). Now a successful businesswoman, she is married to an American TV millionaire and has one son.

Martine Beswick, who portrayed Bond's Bahamian assistant Paula Catlin, was the first girl to hold the distinction of appearing in two Bond films as different characters – and be involved with 007 on both occasions. Her first Bond appearance was in *From Russia With Love* (1963) as the fighting gypsy girl Zora. Martine has also appeared in *One Million Years BC* (1966), *Slave Girls* (1967), *Dr. Jekyll and Sister Hyde* (1971) and *The Happy Hooker Goes to Hollywood* (1980). She has also made numerous appearances in TV features such as *Falcon Crest* (1985). She now resides in England.

Domino, the pawn in Largo's game of nuclear blackmail, was portrayed as a vulnerable plaything by Claudine Auger.

ABOVE: *(left) Martine Beswick sports a tasselled bikini – the kind that's never meant to get wet!*
(right) Another series of publicity shots with no bearing on the actress's role in the film
had Martine taking on a band of SPECTRE frogmen.

Her 5ft 8in 37-25-37 figure helped win her the title of Miss France at the tender age of 15. Later she came to England, where she was an au pair for a London family. The film-makers eventually chose Claudine from a short list of four actresses who had been drawn from 600 possible girls – one of whom had been Raquel Welch. When Claudine's family heard of her winning the role it was her sister Anne-Marie who was most impressed – her bedroom was plastered with pictures of her

favourite star, Sean Connery! Claudine is still friendly with Connery, who, she says, 'was just like a big brother to me' during filming. Her first screen appearance was in *Le Testament d'Orphée* in 1959. She has also appeared in *Triple Cross* (1966), *The Crimebuster* (1977) and *The Associate* (1982), and in advertisements for the French Concorde. She has now generally retired from acting, although she did guest star in the Granada TV series *The Memoirs of Sherlock Holmes* (1993). Claudine is married to a British-based businessman and commutes regularly between London and Paris.

ABOVE: *(top) 'Thunderbirds' Luciana Paluzzi, Claudine Auger and Martine Beswick soak up the sun in the Bahamas. (left) 'Girls on top!' Fiona (Luciana Paluzzi) has Bond just where she wants him. (right) A bad girl who enjoyed being bad, Luciana Paluzzi as Fiona Volpe.*

You Only Live Twice (1967)

JAMES BOND	SEAN CONNERY
AKI	AKIKO WAKABAYASHI
KISSY	MIE HAMA
TIGER TANAKA	TETSURO TAMBA
MR OSATO	TERU SHIMADA
HELGA BRANDT	KARIN DOR
BLOFELD	DONALD PLEASENCE
M	BERNARD LEE
MISS MONEYPENNY	LOIS MAXWELL
Q	DESMOND LLEWELYN

PRODUCERS	HARRY SALTZMAN
	ALBERT R. BROCCOLI
DIRECTOR	LEWIS GILBERT
SCREENPLAY	ROALD DAHL
PRODUCTION DESIGNER	KEN ADAM
DIRECTOR OF PHOTOGRAPHY	FREDDIE YOUNG

JAMES BOND travels to Japan to combat SPECTRE's plot to start World War III from their base inside a hollow volcano.

James Bond reports to M on board a nuclear submarine, fresh from his own 'funeral' at sea. 'Now that you're dead perhaps some of your old friends will leave you alone,' says M.

An American space capsule has been hijacked by an intruder spacecraft and the Americans suspect the Russians. World peace is balanced on a knife edge, and Bond has to work fast to discover the base of the renegade spacecraft as another American launch is imminent.

Once on the Japanese mainland, Bond is contacted by Aki at a Sumo hall and is driven to meet his contact, Henderson, in Tokyo. Henderson, however, is murdered before he can finish briefing the British agent, but Bond crashes through a paper wall and catches the assassin, killing him with his own knife. Seeing the assassin's driver waiting for his return, Bond disguises himself in the dead man's clothes and crawls into the back seat of the car feigning injury. The driver takes him to a large modern building, the offices of Osato Chemicals. Carrying Bond on his shoulder, the driver enters an office and places the impostor on a couch. 'Good evening' smiles Bond, quickly drawing his gun, but the driver is quicker, and throws Bond through the paper walls. Bond fights for his life as he is thrown all over the office, and threatened with decapitation with a Samurai sword. He eventually finishes the bout by smashing the driver over the head with a large stone statuette. Bond notices that a panel covering the safe door is open and decides to investigate. Using an automatic safe-cracking device,

ABOVE: *(right) 'I give you very best duck!' says Ling (Tsai Chin), as the bed in which 007 is taking a post-coital break flips vertically into the wall. (left) Cars and girls – inseparable ingredients of a James Bond movie: here Akiko Wakabayashi does her Bond Girl thing on the bonnet of a Toyota 2000GT.*

ABOVE: *This shot of Karin Dor collects the kitsch prize for the daftest (but fun) publicity shot ever*
taken for a James Bond movie.

is introduced to Osato's confidential secretary, Helga Brandt, and it is quite apparent that he is recognized as the intruder of the previous night. Osato gives the order to kill Bond and as 007 leaves the building he is shadowed by a car full of gunmen who open fire on him. Once again Aki rushes to the rescue in her sports car and the gunmen follow in hot pursuit. Aki radios Tiger asking for the 'usual reception' for the gunmen, and suddenly a helicopter swoops down and lifts the attackers' car into the air on the end of a large magnet, then promptly drops them in Tokyo Bay. 'Just a drop in the ocean,' says Bond.

Aki and Bond drive to Kobe docks, where the *Ning-Po* is berthed and where they are promptly attacked by dock workers in Osato's pay. Bond tells Aki to escape while he fights off their pursuers. After eluding his attackers, Bond is suddenly knocked out from behind. On regaining consciousness, he finds himself tied to a chair aboard the *Ning-Po* with Helga Brandt threatening him with a scalpel. He convinces her that he is an industrial spy and they can share the profit of his night raid on Osato's safe. She cuts him free, and he returns the favour by cutting the straps on her dress, saying, 'Oh, the things I do for England!' Helga pretends that she will fly him to Tokyo, but bails out of the plane leaving Bond to his fate. Luckily, 007 is able to land the aircraft before it explodes in a mass of flames.

Bond rejoins Tiger and Aki and learns that they have discovered the island destination of the *Ning-Po*. The autogyro, *Little Nellie*, has arrived, along with her father. 'Welcome to Japan, Dad,' Bond tells Q, who isn't impressed with 007's juvenile quips. 'I have much curiosity Bond-san,' says a very puzzled Tanaka, 'What is *Little Nellie*?' 'Oh, she's very small, quite fast, she can do anything. Quite your type really,' says

Bond successfully opens the safe but sets off an alarm in the process. Grabbing a handful of documents, he escapes from the pursuing guards with the help of Aki in her Toyota sports car.

Bond wants some answers, but before he can get Aki to talk he has to catch her. She runs into the deserted subway until Bond catches up with her, but then mysteriously stands her ground. As Bond walks towards her the ground opens up beneath his feet and he finds himself hurtling down a metal chute. He is dumped unceremoniously in an armchair at the end of the chute. 'Welcome Bond-san. I am so very pleased to meet you.' Bond has stumbled into the secret underground office of Tiger Tanaka – head of the Japanese Secret Service – and Aki is his top agent. When examining the documents stolen from Osato's safe they find a link with the ship *Ning-Po*. Bond retires with Tiger to his house, where he receives his first 'civilized' bath.

The next day Bond returns to Osato's office posing as Mr Fisher, the managing director of Empire Chemicals. Bond

ABOVE: *(left) A rarely seen publicity shot showcasing the exceptional beauty of Akiko Wakabayashi.*
(right) Bond (Sean Connery) undergoes the transformation into a Japanese and pretends
to take Kissy (Mie Hama) as his wife.

Bond. 007 takes to the skies over the island in the autogyro, and while investigating the volcanoes discovers that he has company in the form of four SPECTRE helicopters. Using his flying arsenal he successfully destroys the enemy aircraft and flies to meet Tiger at the Ninja training school. Bond is then transformed into a Japanese by Tiger's bath girls in readiness for his trip to the Ama island. During the night a SPECTRE assassin kills Aki when poison meant for Bond drips on to her lips. Bond shoots the attacker dead, but he is too late to save Aki.

Meanwhile, inside SPECTRE's headquarters, Blofeld summons Osato and Helga Brandt before him. They have allowed James Bond to escape and someone must pay. Blofeld presses a foot pedal under his desk and Helga falls to her doom, to be consumed by a shoal of voracious piranhas.

Bond is 'married' to Tiger's agent Kissy Suzuki, and they travel to the Ama diving island of Matsu. That night Bond and Kissy are awoken with Tiger's news that the Americans have brought their launch date forward to midnight.

Investigating a grotto where a diving girl has recently been found dead, Bond and Kissy are forced to swim for their lives when Bond realizes that the cavern is full of poison gas. Making their way to the top of the volcano, they are puzzled to see a helicopter descending into its crater. Reaching the edge of

the crater, Bond tests the depth of the lake, only to find it is made of metal. As Bond begins to walk across the false lake the surface starts to slide back to reveal SPECTRE'S headquarters. Kissy makes her way back down the volcano to fetch Tiger and his Ninjas, while Bond enters the headquarters with the aid of rubber suction cups strapped to his hands and knees. Attempting to take the place of a SPECTRE astronaut, Bond is captured and brought before Blofeld.

'They told me you were assassinated in Hong Kong,' Blofeld says smugly. 'Yes. This is my second life,' retorts Bond, looking death in the face. 'You only live twice, Mr Bond,' says Blofeld with an eerie ring of finality.

Tiger and his Ninjas appear in the crater just after the blast-off of the intruder rocket and are met with a hail of automatic gunfire. Bond manages to open the crater roof for a short time to give the Ninjas a fighting chance. One Ninja manages to attach a limpet mine to the crater which blows a gaping hole in the roof. The remainder of Tiger's force then abseil into the volcano, where they engage SPECTRE's forces in a final battle. Blofeld escapes from the control room, taking Bond and Osato with him. After shooting Osato, Blofeld takes aim at Bond, but a well-aimed Ninja throwing star from Tiger finds its mark, and the wounded Blofeld escapes in his monorail. Bond has to get to the exploder button in the

ABOVE: *Following a helicopter into an extinct volcano crater,*
Bond and Kissy are surprised to find the chopper has disappeared.

control room to destroy the intruder spacecraft, but first he must get past Hans, Blofeld's massive bodyguard. Hans delivers a crashing blow to Bond's face, but without serious damage, and eventually Bond despatches him into the ever hungry jaws of the piranhas. Racing into the blazing control room, Bond destroys the intruder spacecraft and averts World War III. Meanwhile, Blofeld sets off an explosive chain reaction in order to destroy his base with the intruders inside. Bond, Kissy, Tiger and the surviving Ninjas run for their lives with the volcano exploding around them. Swimming out to sea, Bond and Kissy clamber into a rubber dinghy as Blofeld's headquarters disappear in a volcanic eruption. As Bond embraces Kissy, M's submarine emerges from the sea under their dinghy.

BORN IN Tokyo on 20 November 1943, Mie Hama started earning her living as a bus conductress at the age of 16. She was considered tall by Japanese standards at 5ft 4½in and had been a contract artist at Toho Studios since she was 17. The most photographed girl in her country, she was often described as the Japanese Brigitte Bardot. Her 35-23-35 figure graced countless homespun movies before appearing as Kissy Suzuki. She continues to appear in TV and films in Japan.

Another contract player at Toho Studios, Akiko Wakabayashi, had played policewomen, secret agents and spies in countless Japanese films prior to her role as Aki. Half an inch shorter than her colleague, Akiko's 35-23-35½ figure was also seen in the Italian film *Le Orientale* (1959), where she played a diving girl, and in the German production of *Haruka Naru Neppu*.

Osato's confidential secretary, Karin Dor, added another role to her long line of character parts. Born in Wiesbaden, Germany, she made her debut at 16 in *The Silent Angel* opposite Christine Kaufmann. She was known as 'Miss Crime' in her homeland because of the countless gangster films in which she appeared – although always as a good girl. A busy and much travelled actress, she has worked in Germany, Italy, Spain and Yugoslavia. She also appeared in *The Face of Fu Manchu* (1965) opposite Christopher Lee, and *Topaz* (1969).

ABOVE: *(left) For Mie Hama, filming in 100-degree heat on the rim of the volcano crater dressed in a bikini was no great discomfort, but matching the location on D Stage at Pinewood in November in the same bikini was a different story – the poor girl literally turned blue! (right) Mie in the warmer climes of Pinewood's stills studio.*
OPPOSITE: *Akiko Wakabayashi's character in* You Only Live Twice *was originally called Suki, but was soon changed to Aki, as everyone on set called her by her abbreviated name.*

On Her Majesty's Secret Service
(1969)

JAMES BOND	GEORGE LAZENBY
TRACY	DIANA RIGG
BLOFELD	TELLY SAVALAS
DRACO	GABRIELE FERZETTI
IRMA BUNT	ILSE STEPPAT
SIR HILARY BRAY	GEORGE BAKER
M	BERNARD LEE
MISS MONEYPENNY	LOIS MAXWELL
Q	DESMOND LLEWELYN
PRODUCERS	HARRY SALTZMAN
	ALBERT R. BROCCOLI
DIRECTOR	PETER HUNT
SCREENPLAY	RICHARD MAIBAUM
DIRECTOR OF PHOTOGRAPHY	MICHAEL REED
PRODUCTION DESIGNER	SYD CAIN

THE WORLD food supply is under threat from bacteriological sabotage and James Bond is once more on the trail of Ernst Stavro Blofeld.

On a coastal road in Portugal, Bond's car is overtaken at speed by a car driven by a beautiful woman. Further down the coast he notices the same woman walking fully clothed into the sea. Realizing that she is attempting suicide, Bond races to the sea's edge and plucks her from a watery grave. Lifting her on to

ABOVE: *(top) James Bond (George Lazenby) rescues Tracy (Diana Rigg) from a watery grave when she attempts suicide. (bottom) Tracy recklessly gambles for high stakes although she has no money. As usual, 007 comes to the rescue.*

ABOVE: *Diana Rigg wearing the 'suicide' scene dress, designed by Marjory Cornelius, and which Diana also wore for her appearance on* The Morecambe and Wise Show.

the sand, he is surprised by two men. The woman is dragged back to her car while Bond is ordered to lie down in a fishing boat. As one man levels his gun to shoot, Bond throws a grappling hook from the boat at him and a vicious fight ensues in the surf and on the beach. Having dealt with both men, Bond is left holding the woman's shoes as she races off in her car. Bond checks into his hotel and is surprised to find that the woman from the beach is also staying there. After paying her gambling debt at the casino, he discovers that she is the Comtessa Teresa di Vicenzo – but her friends call her Tracy. She invites Bond to her room, but on entering he is surprised by a powerful black assailant whom he knocks cold. Returning to his own room, Bond finds Tracy ready to repay her debt. After a night of lovemaking Bond wakes to find that Tracy has gone. She has left a rose and some gambling chips on the pillow – he has been paid in full.

Leaving the hotel for a game of golf, Bond is interrupted by the men he fought on the beach and taken to a demolition yard, where he meets Marc Ange Draco, Tracy's father and head of a Mafia-type organization, the Union Corse. Draco explains to Bond that Tracy has been an awkward and unhappy child since the death of her mother, and that he fears for her life due to her fragile mental state. He feels Bond is the kind of man who could give her the stability she desperately needs, and offers him a million pounds if he will marry her. Bond tells Draco he doesn't need the money and, apart from that, a wife would be a liability for a man in his profession. Draco tempts Bond with information about the whereabouts of Blofeld, telling him he wouldn't tell Her Majesty's Secret Service, but he would tell his future son-in-law. Bond agrees to go along to Draco's birthday celebrations, which Tracy always attends. Realizing that Bond has only attended the party to gather information, Tracy forces her father to tell Bond what he wants

to know. She runs off feeling she has been used yet again, but 007 goes after her, and a real bond of affection is formed between them in the following weeks.

Armed with the knowledge that Blofeld has been dealing with a lawyer in Berne called Gumbold, Bond leaves for Switzerland. He discovers that Blofeld has been using Gumbold as a go-between with the Royal College of Arms in London in his attempt to establish his right to the title of Count de Bleuchamp. He is expecting a visit from one Sir Hilary Bray on the matter.

With the cooperation of the College of Arms, Bond impersonates Sir Hilary and travels to Blofeld's mountain-top hideaway – Piz Gloria. Bond is introduced to Blofeld and is

ABOVE: *(top) Blofeld's Angels of Death in the attractive shape of (left to right) Sylvana Henriques, Julie Ege, Joanna Lumley, Jenny Hanley.*
(bottom) Although there was much talk in the tabloid press of a feud between Lazenby and Rigg during filming,
this was, as one has come to expect, completely untrue.

accepted as the representative of the College. However, when he is caught seducing several of the beautiful girls at Blofeld's Institute of Physiological Research, including Ruby and Nancy, he is exposed as agent 007. Blofeld explains that the girls are his angels of death, and that once returned to their own countries they will administer deadly bacteria into the food chain by a secret method. Bond asks Blofeld how many millions he plans to extort this time, and is amused to find that Blofeld's request is for little more than a recognition to the title of Count and amnesty for his past crimes.

Bond later discovers the manner in which the angels of death are to administer their deadly bacteria. While under hypnosis, the girls have been given their instructions as well as a compact and atomizer as going-away Christmas presents. The gifts contain a receiver and the bacteria. Blofeld will trigger the girls simultaneously to administer the virus. Knowing he must get this information urgently to London, Bond steals some skis and escapes down the mountainside with, hot on his heels, Blofeld's pursuing guards. Managing to reach a small town in the valley, Bond is pleasantly surprised to find Tracy has followed him there. She helps him escape from his pursuers, and, running into a snowstorm, they seek refuge for the night in a barn. The next morning Blofeld and his guards reach the barn, but too late. When Blofeld spots them skiing down the mountain he sends his guards to head them off at the precipice. Bond manages to escape but Blofeld causes a tremendous avalanche which engulfs Tracy. Blofeld's men drag Tracy from the snow.

M refuses to help rescue Tracy and Bond telephones Draco to ask him if he is interested in a demolition job. Flying out of the alpine dawn in helicopters, Bond and Draco attack Blofeld's headquarters in force. Inside Tracy fights for her life against Blofeld's henchmen, despatching one with a champagne bottle and impaling the other on a set of ornamental spikes. Bond rushes into the laboratory looking for Blofeld, while Draco's men set explosive charges to destroy the complex. Tracy, who does not want to leave without Bond, is manhandled into a helicopter by her father. Still searching for Blofeld, Bond is surprised from behind when the SPECTRE chief opens fire on him with a machine-gun. Both Blofeld and Bond leap from the building as the explosive charges destroy the institute. Chasing Blofeld down a toboggan run, Bond is blown off course by a hand grenade thrown at him by the fleeing man. Managing to leap on to Blofeld's toboggan, Bond struggles furiously with him until the SPECTRE chief becomes caught in the low-hanging bough of a tree.

James Bond is reunited with Tracy at her father's ranch in Portugal – it is their wedding day! M, Moneypenny and Q are all in attendance to wish the happy couple good luck. Q hasn't always seen eye to eye with 007 but says, 'If there's anything you ever need.' 'Thank you, Q,' replies Bond, 'but this time I've got the gadgets, and I know how to use them.'

ABOVE: *(top) Bond and Tracy's wedding day takes place on her father's estate in Portugal.*
(below) Olympe (Virginia North), Marc Ange Draco's very personal secretary.

Mr and Mrs Bond leave for their honeymoon in their flower-adorned Aston Martin. A little way into their journey Bond stops on a mountain road to remove the flowers. Suddenly without warning machine-gun fire from a passing Mercedes strafes their car. 'It's Blofeld,' shouts Bond, leaping into the car. Only then does he realize that Tracy is dead.

He cradles her softly in his arms, weeping, 'We have all the time in the world.'

THE FILM follows Fleming's writing very closely and in essence the women in the film are the characters in his novel.

With the casting of an inexperienced actor in the role of James Bond, it was important that the leading lady was a seasoned actress, and Diana Rigg was certainly a good choice. Her portrayal of Tracy as Bond's equal brought a freshness and vitality to the part, and is probably her best movie performance. Diana came to Bond fresh from TV's *The Avengers* and this is reflected in her fight scenes in *On Her Majesty's Secret Service*. Other appearances include, *The Assassination Bureau* (1968) with Oliver Reed, *The Hospital* (1971) with George C. Scott and *Theatre of Blood* (1973) with Vincent Price. Her first love is the theatre, where she has achieved considerable success in such roles as Heloise in *Abelard and Heloise* (1970), *Lady Macbeth* (1971), Eliza Doolittle in *Pygmalion* (1974) and more recently in Stephen Sondheim's *Follies* and the Greek tragedy *Medea*. She was awarded a CBE in the late 1980s and the title of Dame in 1994.

Angela Scoular appeared as Bond's bedtime partner Ruby. She has appeared in TV productions such as *Penmarric*, and her varied stage roles have included Ophelia to Alan Bates's *Hamlet*. Her films include *Casino Royale* (1967), *Here We Go Round the Mulberry Bush* (1967) and *Great Catherine* (1968). She is married to the actor Leslie Phillips.

Catherine Von Schell played Nancy, Bond's other bedmate at Piz Gloria, who beat Blofeld's curfew to bag Bond. Her other appearances include *Moon Zero Two* (1969) and TV's *Space 1999*.

'Of course I know what he's allergic to!' is the bitchy line delivered by Joanna Lumley when Bond masquerades as Sir Hilary Bray. Joanna found success in TV's *The New Avengers* after her appearance with Bond and earlier TV successes have been followed by the acclaimed comedy series *Absolutely Fabulous*. In 1995, she was awarded the OBE.

ABOVE: *Ruby Bartlett (Angela Scoular) from Lancashire discovers that Bond wears his kilt in traditional fashion.*
OPPOSITE: *Nancy (Catherine Von Schell) is able to beat Blofeld's curfew with the aid of her nailfile, and visit Bond for an enervating evening 'studying genealogy'.*

Diamonds Are Forever (1971)

JAMES BOND	SEAN CONNERY
TIFFANY CASE	JILL ST. JOHN
BLOFELD	CHARLES GRAY
PLENTY O'TOOLE	LANA WOOD
WILLARD WHYTE	JIMMY DEAN
SAXBY	BRUCE CABOT
MR KIDD	PUTTER SMITH
MR WINT	BRUCE GLOVER
LEITER	NORMAN BURTON
M	BERNARD LEE
Q	DESMOND LLEWELYN
MISS MONEYPENNY	LOIS MAXWELL
PRODUCERS	HARRY SALTZMAN
	ALBERT R. BROCCOLI
DIRECTOR	GUY HAMILTON
SCREENPLAY	RICHARD MAIBAUM
	TOM MANKIEWICZ
DIRECTOR OF PHOTOGRAPHY	TED MOORE
PRODUCTION DESIGNER	KEN ADAM

JAMES BOND battles again with Blofeld – and his doubles – when he holds the world to ransom with a diamond reflected laser orbiting in space.

Discovering Blofeld's whereabouts, Bond infiltrates his headquarters and, after disposing of his bodyguards, despatches him smartly to his death in a pool of boiling mud. 'Welcome to hell, Blofeld,' says Bond as the SPECTRE chief's body sinks below the surface.

With the death of 'Blofeld', Bond is able to concentrate on his next mission. Visiting the London headquarters of a diamond syndicate, Bond and M learn from Sir Donald Munger that a large number of diamonds are going missing from a South African mining operation. Unusually, the diamonds are not turning up on the black market. Someone is stockpiling them, and Bond is given the job of discovering who is organizing the smuggling pipeline and why.

Assuming the identity of professional smuggler Peter Franks, Bond travels to Amsterdam and makes contact with Tiffany Case, the next link in the chain. Bond learns that Tiffany was named after the famous store in New York, where her mother gave birth to her while shopping for a wedding ring. 'Well, I'm glad for your sake that it wasn't Van Cleef and Arpels,' remarks Bond. Back at his hotel Bond learns from Q that the real Peter Franks has killed his guard and escaped. Rushing back to Tiffany's apartment, Bond intercepts Franks at the front door of the building. Moving into the elevator, Bond tries to overpower him and a fierce struggle ensues. Arriving at Tiffany's floor, Bond and Franks fall from the elevator,

ABOVE: (left) Marie (Denise Perrier, Miss World 1953) holds the key to the whereabouts of Ernst Stavro Blofeld. And 007 will go to any lengths to get the information.
(right) When Lady Luck deserts you at the crap table, so does Plenty O'Toole (Lana Wood).

ABOVE: *Jill St. John as Tiffany Case was the first American actress to be cast as a Bond Girl.*

The next morning Bond and Felix Leiter's men are given the slip by Tiffany when she disappears with the real gems. Bond goes to Tiffany's house, where he finds Plenty dead in her swimming pool wearing one of Tiffany's wigs. Wint and Kidd have killed her believing it's Tiffany. Bond forces Tiffany to tell him where she has left the diamonds. Establishing the gems are now in the possession of Dr Metz, Bond and Tiffany follow him to Willard Whyte's Techtronics Factory. Once inside, Bond observes Metz's technicians constructing a curious-looking machine. Bond is soon recognized as an intruder, and he clambers over an artificial moonscape to escape in a nearby moon-buggy. Bond and Tiffany return to the streets of Las Vegas

knocking a fire extinguisher from the wall. Bond grabs the extinguisher, sprays it in Franks' face and knocks him into the stairwell to his death. Switching wallets with the dead man, Bond drags the corpse into Tiffany's apartment, where she searches the body for identification. 'Oh, my God, you've just killed James Bond,' squeals Tiffany, brandishing Bond's Playboy Club card. 'Is that who it is?' says Bond, feigning indifference. 'Well, it just proves no one is indestructible.'

Hiding the diamonds in Franks' body, Bond and Tiffany fly to Las Vegas, where Bond is collected by a hearse full of gangsters. Posing as Franks' brother, Bond is driven to Slumber Incorporated funeral home, where the diamonds are separated from the body during its cremation. Bond is knocked unconscious by gay killers Wint and Kidd, and placed in a coffin which they send into the flames of the crematorium. But when the diamonds are discovered to be fake, Morton Slumber opens the coffin and demands to know what Bond has done with the real gems. Bond climbs out of the still-smoking coffin and heads for the Tropicana Hotel, where he later visits the casino. 'Hi there, I'm Plenty, Plenty O'Toole,' comes a voice from Bond's side at the crap table. 'Named after your father perhaps,' replies Bond, viewing the girl's obvious charms. Collecting their winnings, Plenty and Bond retire to his room but are interrupted by three gunmen who proceed to throw Plenty out of the window. 'Exceptionally fine shot,' says Bond as Plenty lands safely in the swimming pool ten floors below. 'I didn't know there was a pool down there,' replies the gunman as Bond knocks him to the floor. To Bond's astonishment the gunmen retreat, dragging their unconscious colleague with them. Bond then realizes that Tiffany is waiting for him in the bedroom.

ABOVE: (left) 007 (Sean Connery) will use any device to get the information he wants, and what better device than Marie's bikini top! (right) James Bond (Sean Connery), the high roller, soon attracts a Vegas vamp in the voluptuous shape of Plenty O'Toole.

only to be chased by the local police force. Bond resourcefully escapes by taking his car up on two wheels and down a narrow alleyway.

After resting with Tiffany on a water bed filled with fish, Bond decides to visit the mysterious millionaire, Willard Whyte. Climbing from the window he hitches a ride on top of the outside of the elevator, which takes him to Whyte's penthouse suite. After mountaineering on the outside of the building, Bond finally gains entry to the suite via the skylight. Once inside he is greeted by a familiar voice, 'Good evening, Mr Bond,' and sees Blofeld at his desk. Then – 'Good evening, 007.' Bond is amazed to see a second Blofeld walk down the staircase towards him. 'Double jeopardy, Mr Bond.' Bond remembers that he still has his bolt-firing gun, but he does not know which Blofeld to kill. A white cat walks into the room and Bond sees an answer to his problem. Bond steps on the cat and it jumps into the arms of one of the Blofelds. Bond fires a bolt into the head of the Blofeld with the cat. Another white cat enters the room, but this one has a diamond necklace

ABOVE: *(top) 'High there I'm Plenty, Plenty O'Toole.' 'Named after your father perhaps.'*
(bottom) Bond and Tiffany Case chill out on a fish-filled waterbed at the Whyte House.

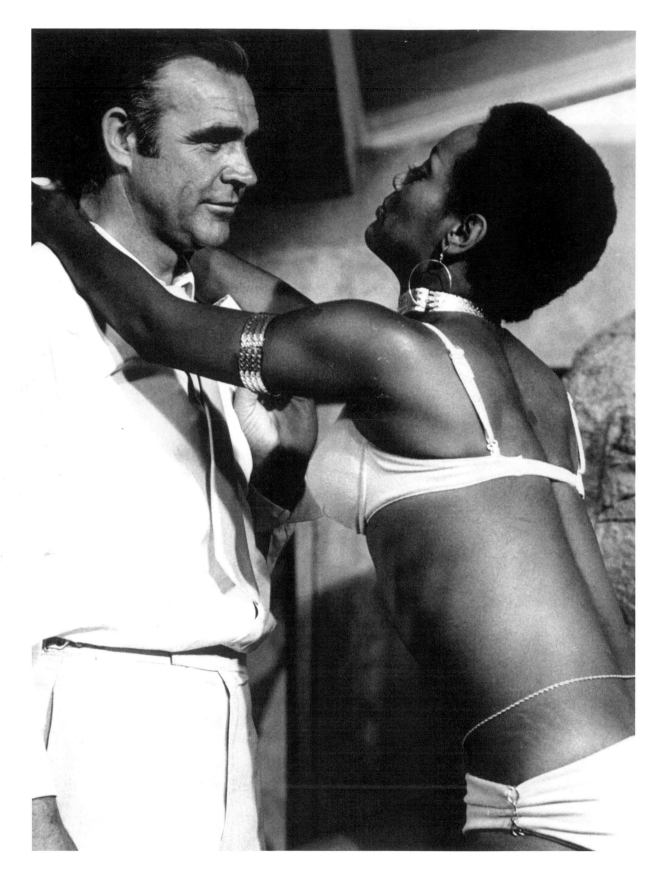

ABOVE: *Bond is in for a painful surprise from Willard Whyte's bodyguard, Thumper (Trina Parks).*

around its neck. 'Right idea,' says the surviving Blofeld. 'But wrong pussy,' replies Bond. Blofeld ushers Bond into an elevator down to the basement where gas escapes from a grille in the floor. Bond falls unconscious and is thrown into the boot of a waiting car by Wint and Kidd. Left for dead in an underground pipe, Bond manages to escape and leads Felix Leiter and his men to Willard Whyte, kept prisoner in his desert home by Blofeld, but not before being thrown all over the place by Bambi and Thumper. Meanwhile Tiffany has been kidnapped by Blofeld, whom she spotted making his escape dressed as a woman.

Blofeld launches his satellite, and the reason why he required such a huge quantity of diamonds becomes apparent. He has had the gems fitted to a reflector dish on the orbiting spacecraft, and is now in control of a laser of unparalleled power, able to strike anywhere on earth. To demonstrate the awesome power of the laser, Blofeld causes the destruction of a Russian submarine, an American spacecraft and a Chinese missile site. By the process of elimination, Bond discovers that Blofeld is hiding on an oil rig off the coast of California.

Arriving in a parachuted balloon which 'walks' on water Bond is taken aboard the rig. Bond finds Blofeld gloating over his new mistress, Tiffany, who is stretched out on the couch. Blofeld then takes Bond on a guided tour of the control room which gives 007 the opportunity to switch the tape that directs the satellite. Unfortunately, Tiffany, not realizing Bond has already switched the tape – switches it back again. Bond is thrown in the brig, but on the way is able to release a nearby weather balloon, which is the signal for Felix and Willard Whyte to attack in a fleet of helicopters. The rig is destroyed in an aerial attack while Bond uses the mini-sub containing an escaping Blofeld as a battering-ram to destroy the control room.

Safely aboard the *Queen Mary*, Bond and Tiffany indulge in a romantic evening but are interrupted by the appearance of two waiters bearing food and drink with the compliments of Willard Whyte. Although Bond has never actually seen Wint and Kidd he realizes that he is in danger when he recognizes Wint's overpowering perfume. Wint grabs Bond from behind as Kidd moves menacingly towards him holding flaming shish kebabs. Bond breaks a bottle of brandy and throws its contents at Kidd. Engulfed in flames, Kidd jumps overboard. Still struggling with Wint, Bond picks up the bomb that has fallen out of the 'bombe surprise', tucks it between the killer's legs and sends him somersaulting over the side of the ship exploding in mid-air. 'Well, he certainly left with his tail tucked between his legs.'

Looking up at the stars, Tiffany turns to Bond and asks, 'James, how the hell do we get those diamonds down from there?'

JILL ST. JOHN (real name Jill Oppenheim) was the first American actress to play a leading Bond girl. Born in 1940, she made her screen debut in *Summer Love* (1958), and other roles followed in *The Lost World* (1960), *The Liquidator* (1965), *Tony Rome* (1967) and *Sitting Target* (1972). She has made numerous appearances on American TV series, including *Brenda Starr, Girl Reporter* (1974) and *Hart to Hart* (1979) with husband Robert Wagner. She had a regular cooking slot on *Good Morning America* and published *The Jill St. John Cookbook*. She is an accomplished skier and owns a boutique in Aspen, Colorado.

Lana Wood is probably best known for being the sister of the late Natalie Wood. Her appearances have been mostly limited to American TV shows, including *Peyton Place, Long Hot Summer* and *Capitol*. She was featured in John Ford's Western *The Searchers* (1956) playing her teenage sister Natalie as a child.

ABOVE: *For your thighs only! Bambi (Donna Garratt) gets a vice-like grip on Bond (Sean Connery).*

Live And Let Die (1973)

JAMES BOND	ROGER MOORE
SOLITAIRE	JANE SEYMOUR
DR. KANANGA	YAPHET KOTTO
SHERIFF PEPPER	CLIFTON JAMES
TEE HEE	JULIUS W. HARRIS
BARON SAMEDI	GEOFFREY HOLDER
ROSIE	GLORIA HENDRY
FELIX LEITER	DAVID HEDISON
M	BERNARD LEE
MISS MONEYPENNY	LOIS MAXWELL
PRODUCERS	HARRY SALTZMAN
	ALBERT R. BROCCOLI
DIRECTOR	GUY HAMILTON
SCREENPLAY	TOM MANKIEWICZ
DIRECTOR OF PHOTOGRAPHY	TED MOORE
SUPERVISING ART DIRECTOR	SYD CAIN

JAMES BOND battles against drug king Dr Kananga and his voodoo henchmen in his attempt to create a nation of drug dependants.

Following the murder of three British agents in 24 hours, James Bond receives an early morning visit from M and Miss Moneypenny. Quickly hiding Miss Caruso, an agent involved in his recent Italian mission, in his wardrobe, Bond is briefed by M and leaves for New York to investigate the killings. But he still finds time first to use his magnetic watch to unfasten the zip on Miss Caruso's dress.

In New York Bond is en route to meet his old friend CIA agent Felix Leiter, when an attempt is made on his life. Meeting with Leiter, Bond learns that he is keeping Dr Kananga, the president of the small Caribbean island of San Monique, under observation. Leiter continues his surveillance, while Bond traces his would-be assassin's car to Harlem and a restaurant called the Fillet of Soul. Once inside, Bond finds himself trapped. He has fallen into the hands of Harlem gangster Mr Big and his henchman Tee Hee. Sitting at the table dealing tarot cards is Solitaire, who, with the gift of second sight, has predicted Bond's arrival. Mr Big gives the order that the 'honky' should be wasted, and two of his men take Bond

ABOVE: *(left) In Dr Kananga's underground lair, Solitaire (Jane Seymour) and Bond (Roger Moore) are given the 'condemned man ate a hearty breakfast' routine. (right) Madeline Smith cuts an impressive figure as Italian secret agent Miss Caruso.*

ABOVE: *Jane Seymour perfectly conveyed the naïve virginal qualities that made*
Solitaire such an attractive conquest to Bond.

outside. After a brief struggle Bond eludes the killers and meets CIA agent Harold Strutter, who has been trailing him.

Leaving New York, Bond follows Kananga to Jamaica, where he finds 'Mrs Bond' waiting for him in his hotel room. She is CIA agent Rosie Carver. With the help of Quarrel Junior, Rosie promises to show Bond where one of the agents was killed. But Bond discovers she is in the pay of Kananga, and Rosie, running scared, is shot and killed by one of the Doctor's robot scarecrows. Kananga is relying on Solitaire's psychic powers to keep several steps ahead of Bond's movements, and cannot understand her sudden change of mood. In fact, unknown to Kananga, Solitaire has foreseen in the cards that she and Bond will become lovers.

During the night Bond gains entrance to Kananga's clifftop home with the aid of a hang-glider. Once inside, he confronts Solitaire, who is reading the tarot. Bond tricks her into bed using a tarot pack stacked in his favour – every card in the deck is the Lovers. The following morning, seemingly unconcerned that Solitaire has lost her powers along with her virginity, Bond dutifully goes in search of Kananga's deadly secret. He finds it – poppy fields. Acre upon acre of poppy fields cover the hillside under camouflage netting, and Bond realizes that they must be destroyed before Kananga can harvest his deadly crop. However, Bond and Solitaire are spotted by an enemy helicopter, which opens fire on them with machine-guns. Running for their lives, they commandeer an old double-decker bus to escape their pursuers, who are now chasing them in cars and on motorbikes. Approaching a low-level bridge at high speed, Bond slices off the top of the bus, which conveniently falls on the pursuing car, trapping its occupants. Reaching the harbour safely, Bond and Solitaire escape with Quarrel Junior in his boat. Mr Big wants Solitaire back, and as

ABOVE: *Jane Seymour's character barely looks cheerful throughout the whole movie,*
but during rehearsal she allowed a smile for the stillsman.

the couple are leaving from the local airport, his men capture them. Solitaire creates a diversion, and Bond is chased in and out of the aircraft hangars by Mr Big's men, demolishing many cars and aircraft in the process, but he escapes.

Bond rejoins Felix Leiter in New York, where they visit the local Fillet of Soul restaurant. While Leiter is distracted with a fake telephone call, the floor opens up and Bond disappears into the basement. Bond is once more face to face with Mr Big, Tee Hee and Solitaire. Mr Big asks Bond if he has slept with Solitaire, but, ever the gentleman, Bond refuses to answer to anyone except Kananga. Before Bond's eyes Mr Big's identity is torn away as Kananga appears from under his heavy disguise. He explains that he intends to ensnare the drug population of America by giving away free samples of his heroin, thereby putting all other operators out of business and at the same time greatly increasing the number of addicts. When his poppy fields are harvested, he will increase the price of his goods – and the product can be distributed through his chain of Fillet of Soul restaurants. His employees will be kept in check by Baron Samedi and the threat of voodoo. Bond is knocked unconscious by Tee Hee and taken to a crocodile farm, and as Solitaire is of no further use to him, Kananga decides to concoct a fitting punishment for her.

Arriving at the crocodile farm, Bond learns it is mainly a front for Kananga's drug-refining activities but there are enough of the reptiles about for him to be left as lunch. Ingeniously avoiding his place on the menu, Bond makes his escape from the island running over the backs of the crocodiles. Setting the refining plant on fire, Bond escapes in a high-powered speedboat into the nearby Louisiana bayous. But

ABOVE: (left) Miss Caruso makes a beeline for 007's wardrobe to avoid M and Moneypenny.
(top) Rosie Carver (Gloria Hendry) suggests that Bond wouldn't shoot her after making love.
Bond, ever the lad, replies, 'I certainly wouldn't have killed you before!'
(bottom) A different Bond but, as usual, always a beautiful woman or two on his arm.

Kananga's men and the local red-neck sheriff, J. W. Pepper, are close on his tail. Once again Bond evades capture, but not before numerous boats and police cars are wrecked.

Under cover of night, Bond and Quarrel Junior land on San Monique. Bond rescues Solitaire from a sacrificial ceremony while Quarrel plants explosive charges to destroy the poppy fields. Finding their way into Kananga's subterranean lair, they are overcome by his guards and tied together as bait for his pet sharks. Using the motorized bezel on his wristwatch to cut himself free, Bond faces Kananga in combat. The two men fall into the shark pool, where Bond forces a CO_2 gas pellet into Kananga's mouth, causing the unfortunate man to blow up like a balloon and explode.

With the mission successfully completed, Bond and Solitaire return to New York by overnight train. Unknown to the retiring couple, Tee Hee is also aboard. Breaking into their sleeping-car, Tee Hee attempts to kill Bond with the pincers on his artificial arm. Bond succeeds in jamming Tee Hee's pincers on the window frame before throwing him out of the window. Reacting to Solitaire's muffled cries, Bond pulls the bunk out of the wall where she has been trapped during the fight. 'Now what are you doing?' she asks. 'Just being disarming darling,' replies Bond as he throws Tee Hee's artificial arm out of the window.

The train speeds through the night with Baron Samedi sitting astride the locomotive. Perhaps the man is one of the undead after all.

BOND IS limited to an involvement with only three women in this adventure. Cubby Broccoli had seen Jane Seymour in

ABOVE: *(left) 'Snakes alive!' Having displeased Kananga, Solitaire is offered as the sacrifice in a voodoo ritual. (right & below) Solitaire in her various costumes as high priestess (costumes designed by Julie Harris).*

the BBC TV series *The Onedin Line* and thought that she was the clear choice for the role of the virginal Solitaire. Born in Hillingdon, Middlesex, Jane attended Wimbledon High School until she was 13, when she moved to the Arts Educational School to study ballet. Unfortunately, she developed cartilage trouble and was forced to abandon her chosen career. At 17 she won her first screen role in *Oh! What a Lovely War* (1969) and, after leaving school, appeared in several stage productions, including *The Net* and as Ophelia in *Hamlet*. She was committed to work on *The Onedin Line* when she was cast as Solitaire, but the BBC re-arranged her schedule so she would be free. Although Jane has appeared in films which include *Young Winston* (1972), *Somewhere in Time* (1980) and *Lassiter* (1984), she has become queen of the TV mini-series with appearances in *The Winds of War, East of Eden* and her series *Dr Quinn – Medicine Woman*. She has also appeared advertising a famous perfume and has published her *Guide to Romantic Living*.

Ex-Playboy Bunny Gloria Hendry was seen briefly as double agent Rosie Carver before becoming the obligatory sacrificial lamb in this adventure. Her other appearances include *For Love of Ivy* (1968), *The Landlord* (1970), *Across 110th Street* (1972) and *Black Caesar* (1973).

Seen escaping from a compromising situation as Miss Caruso was Madeline Smith. This childlike British actress has featured in many TV shows, usually cast as an innocent abroad, and her screen career has also reflected this trend, with roles in *Taste the Blood of Dracula* (1969), *The Vampire Lovers* (1970), *Up Pompeii* (1971) and *Frankenstein and the Monster from Hell* (1973).

ABOVE: *(left) The first publicity shot to announce both the new Bond and the new Bond Girl.*
(right) Ex-Playboy Bunny Gloria Hendry made the most of her small role.

The Man With The Golden Gun (1974)

JAMES BOND	ROGER MOORE
SCARAMANGA	CHRISTOPHER LEE
GOODNIGHT	BRITT EKLAND
ANDREA	MAUD ADAMS
NICK NACK	HERVE VILLECHAIZE
J. W. PEPPER	CLIFTON JAMES
HIP	SOON TAIK OH
M	BERNARD LEE
MISS MONEYPENNY	LOIS MAXWELL
Q	DESMOND LLEWELYN
PRODUCERS	HARRY SALTZMAN
	ALBERT R. BROCCOLI
DIRECTOR	GUY HAMILTON
SCREENPLAY	RICHARD MAIBAUM
	TOM MANKIEWICZ
DIRECTORS OF PHOTOGRAPHY	TED MOORE
	OSWALD MORRIS
PRODUCTION DESIGNER	PETER MURTON

JAMES BOND duels with Scaramanga – the man with the golden gun – to win possession of a Solex Agitator and thereby solve the problems of the world's energy shortage.

Entering M's office, Bond learns that a golden bullet sent through the mail has his 007 number engraved on it. M believes the bullet has been sent by million-dollar hit man Scaramanga, and that he has been contracted to kill Bond. M suggests 007 finds Scaramanga before the hired killer finds him. Bond is also told to search for Gibson, a scientist who has disappeared with an invaluable Solex Agitator, a device which enables man to harness energy from the sun.

Bond travels to Beirut to recover the bullet that killed 002, which now graces the navel of belly dancer Saida as a lucky charm. Bond swallows the bullet during a fight with three local thugs, and, discovering it missing, the girl cries, 'I've lost my charm.' 'Not from where I'm standing,' smirks Bond as he leaves her wrecked dressing-room. After examining the bullet, Q decides it could have been made by only one man – Lazar, an infamous Portuguese gun-maker living in Macau. Arriving at Lazar's shop, Bond forces an answer from the shifty

ABOVE: (left) 'Hold on, sir, she's just coming'. Bond (Roger Moore) and Mary Goodnight (Britt Ekland) are about to be interrupted by a phone call from M. (right) More of a sinner than a saint, Roger Moore's 007 is surprised to discover that Andrea Anders (Maud Adams) showers with her gun.

Naval Intelligence are using the old liner as their base, and arresting officer Hip is with the Service. He is surprised to meet both M and Q, and even more surprised to find the dead man was the missing scientist, Gibson. It appears that Gibson was working for Hai Fat, who probably hired Scaramanga to kill the scientist. So Bond travels to Bangkok to confront the wealthy industrialist, gambling on the chance that he has never met the killer.

Arriving at the industrialist's mountainside mansion, Bond encounters an Oriental girl, Chew Mee, swimming naked in the pool. Outraged by Bond's intrusion, Hai Fat asks him to leave, but when Bond opens his shirt to reveal a third nipple, well-known physical abnormality of the real Scaramanga, the industrialist believes him to be the hired killer. Before he leaves, Bond is invited to dinner by Hai Fat. He tells Hip of his dinner date: 'He must have found me quite titillating.'

Bond leaves Goodnight at the hotel and sets out for his appointment. Walking through Hai Fat's gardens, he is set upon by two sumo wrestlers. At first, he seems to be gaining

gun-maker when he points a nearby rifle at the man's groin and quips, 'Speak now or for ever hold your piece.' Not surprisingly, Lazar obliges.

Bond visits the local casino, where Scaramanga's mistress, Andrea Anders, is to collect another consignment of golden bullets. He follows her to Hong Kong but loses her when liaison officer Mary Goodnight inadvertently blocks his exit. Andrea drives off in a green Rolls-Royce. Annoyed at losing his only lead, Bond discovers from Goodnight that there is just one hotel in town which uses green Rolls-Royces as courtesy cars. Entering Andrea's hotel room, Bond surprises her in the shower, and is surprised himself when she produces a gun. 'A water pistol?' asks Bond, unruffled. After manhandling Andrea, Bond discovers that Scaramanga is due to visit the Bottoms Up Club. Bond suggests that Andrea should say nothing about their talk as Scaramanga may even use one of those little golden bullets on her. 'And that would be a pity,' says Bond, 'because they're very expensive.'

A man leaving the Bottoms Up Club is shot dead by Scaramanga. Drawing his Walther PPK, Bond is soon arrested and taken to the partially submerged wreck of the *Queen Elizabeth* in Hong Kong harbour. Once inside, he learns that

ABOVE: *'I've lost my charm!' Bond is about to bite the bullet from Saida (Carmen de Sautoy) the belly dancer's navel when he is set upon by thugs.*

the upper hand, but he is knocked unconscious from behind by the diminutive Nick Nack. Scaramanga's midget manservant is on the point of killing 007 when Hai Fat intervenes. 'Take Mr Bond to school,' he commands. 'Heaven, definitely heaven,' says Bond as he regains consciousness in the arms of several beautiful servant girls. However, he soon realizes that he is far from dead when he is forced into combat against two pupils of Hai Fat's martial arts academy. Bond

jumps through a meshed window, and Hip's two nieces vanquish the pupils. Bond makes for the river, where he steals a boat, chased by the remainder of the pupils. But, surprising them from a side turning, Bond runs through their boat, slicing it in half. When Hai Fat learns of Bond's escape, he decides to lie low but is shot dead by Scaramanga, who tells the dead man's associate, 'Mr Fat has just resigned – I'm the new chairman of the board. He always did like that mausoleum – put him in it!'

Bond meets Goodnight for dinner and is offered a complimentary bottle of Phuyuck '74. 'I approve,' says Bond. 'You do?' says a very surprised Goodnight. 'Oh, not the wine. Your frock. Tight in all the right places, not too many buttons.' Bond raises his glass for a toast. 'To this moment and the moment yet to come.' 'Oh, darling, I'm tempted,' says Goodnight breathlessly, 'but killing a few hours as one of your passing fancies isn't quite my scene.' Goodnight leaves as Bond is observed through binoculars by Nick Nack.

Returning to his hotel room alone and slightly dejected, Bond is pleasantly surprised to find Goodnight dressed in her nightie. 'My hard to get act didn't last very long, did it?' Before Bond and Goodnight are able to consummate their desire, they are interrupted by Andrea. Bond bundles Goodnight into the wardrobe as Andrea explains she has come to warn 007 that Scaramanga knows he is in town, and it was she who sent the bullet to his headquarters. Andrea wants to leave Scaramanga, and Bond is the only man who can kill him and set her free. She tells Bond that Scaramanga talks of him with great admiration and even has a wax likeness of Bond. Determined that Bond should kill Scaramanga, Andrea offers herself to 007 and the couple retire to the bed. Andrea returns to Scaramanga's junk and Bond releases a very angry Goodnight from the wardrobe.

The next day Bond visits a Thai boxing match, where he has arranged to meet Andrea. Sitting next to her, Bond realizes that the girl has been shot through the chest. As Bond rifles the dead girl's handbag searching for the Solex, a tall, dark man occupies the seat next to him – Scaramanga. Bond finds himself held at gun point by Nick Nack, but notices the Solex hidden in the litter on the floor of the boxing hall, and manages to palm it on to the tray of peanuts carried by undercover agent Hip. Scaramanga tells Bond that he has no argument with him and will not harm him if he stays seated until after Scaramanga has left the building. Meanwhile Hip has passed the Solex to Goodnight, who is investigating Scaramanga's car when she is bundled into the boot by the killer.

Unable to hail a taxi, Bond drives a new car through the showroom window, only to find that he is carrying a passenger – Sheriff J. W. Pepper. The sheriff is on vacation in Bangkok and remembers Bond from the destruction he caused in the Louisiana bayous. But as he is on a mission, J. W. decides to help him. Missing a turning that Scaramanga has taken in his car, Bond does a 360-degree roll over a broken bridge to catch up with the killer. 'I've never done that before!' exclaims a breathless Sheriff Pepper as he bounces into the back seat of the car. Neither has Bond! Nevertheless, Scaramanga escapes capture when his car, fitted with wings, takes to the skies.

Scaramanga's car has been found abandoned 200 miles west of Bangkok, and Goodnight's homing signal has been tracked to a small group of islands in Red Chinese waters. M is

ABOVE: *While investigating Hai Fat's estate, Bond spies Chew Mee (Françoise Thilly) swimming naked in the businessman's pool.*

unable to sanction 007 landing in such a delicate area, but Bond decides to pay an unofficial visit. He pilots a seaplane to the island and, on landing, is met by Nick Nack carrying a bottle of champagne. Scaramanga introduces himself by shooting the cork from the bottle of champagne. Entering the hit man's island fortress, Scaramanga shows Bond around his solar energy station, which is overseen by his man Krar. Scaramanga's plan is to sell the Solex to the highest bidder and make untold millions. Showing Bond how he is also able to focus the power through a Solex gun, Scaramanga explodes Bond's seaplane. 'Now that's what I call solar power,' gloats the million-dollar hit man. 'That's what I call trouble,' retorts a worried 007. 'Mr Bond, I am now undeniably the man with the golden gun!' Bond does not argue the point.

Over lunch, Scaramanga explains that he and Bond are much the same, but for the vast difference in their incomes. 'There's a useful four-letter word – and you're full of it!' retorts an angry Bond. 'When I kill it is on the specific orders of my government, and those I kill are themselves killers.' Scaramanga suggests a 'duel of Titans', he and Bond should face each other man to man – his golden gun against 007's Walther PPK. As the two men stand back to back, Nick Nack starts the count. On the count of twenty, Bond turns and fires, but Scaramanga is nowhere to

be seen. Nick Nack leads Bond into the hit man's funhouse, explaining, 'If you kill him all this will be mine. Good shooting, Monsieur Bond.' Disinclined to trust the diminutive manservant, 007 admits, 'I've never killed a midget before, but there can always be a first time!'

Bond is stalked by Scaramanga through the funhouse. Bond loses his PPK as it falls to the bottom of a shaft and, drawn by the noise, Scaramanga closes in for the kill. The hit man is met with a bullet in the chest as the wax effigy that is now Bond turns and shoots him dead. Inside the complex, Bond meets Goodnight, who asks where Scaramanga is. 'Flat on his coup de grâce,' quips 007. Bond discovers that Goodnight has pushed overseer Krar into the helium-cooled tanks, and his body temperature has caused the energy station to dangerously overheat. Bond enters the energy station control room to retrieve the Solex Agitator. Trying to prise the agitator from its housing, 007 is almost incinerated by the solar beam when Goodnight accidentally backs into the control panel, turning on the machine. With the agitator safely in their possession, Bond and Goodnight escape the island as the complex explodes in balls of fire.

Relaxing in the bedroom aboard Scaramanga's junk, Bond and Goodnight are interrupted when Nick Nack slips in through the ceiling. Nick Nack tries to kill

ABOVE: *(left) He was small, but he never forgot: Nick Nack (Herve Villechaize) is given a lift by Britt Ekland and Maud Adams. (right) At the Kung Fu academy, 007 is shown how it should be done by Hip's nieces.*
INSET: *'He has a powerful weapon.' Professional killer Scaramanga (Christopher Lee) 'visits' with Andrea the night before a hit to keep his aim steady.*

Bond with a knife, but is eventually captured by 007 in a large suitcase. Screaming, 'I may be small but I never forget,' from inside the case, Nick Nack is taken up on deck by Bond. He returns, empty-handed, to the cabin and Goodnight asks, 'What did you do with him?' 'What do you think?' replies Bond. 'Oh, James, you didn't?' 'Yes, I damn well did!' retorts an angry Bond. Embracing Goodnight on the bed, Bond is interrupted yet again when M telephones. M asks to speak to Goodnight and Bond asks him to hold on. 'She's just coming, sir!'

The junk sails towards the horizon with a forlorn Nick Nack imprisoned in the crow's nest.

BRITT EKLAND had wanted to appear in a Bond movie for some years and her ambition was realized when Cubby Broccoli cast her as Mary Goodnight after seeing her in *The Wicker Man* (1973). Britt was born in Stockholm, Sweden. Her career started at the age of 15 when she appeared in a toothpaste

commercial. She spent two years in drama school and played small parts in films and on TV and then toured Sweden with a travelling theatre company. Britt speaks Italian, French and German as well as English and her native Swedish. She was married to Peter Sellers in 1964, and was divorced in 1968. Companion to pop singer Rod Stewart through the Seventies, she then married Stray Cats drummer, Slim Jim, but divorced. Her appearances include *The Night They Raided Minsky's* (1968) with Joseph Wiseman, *Get Carter* (1971) with Michael Caine, *The Monster Club* (1980) and *Scandal* (1989). In recent years she has appeared in the theatre in pantomime and farce.

Another native of Sweden is Maud Adams, whose 5ft 9in helped begin her career in modelling. Later, she decided to branch into acting. Studying under Warren Robertson, a top American drama coach, she made her screen debut in *The Christian Licquorice Store* (1970) opposite Beau Bridges. Maud's role as Scaramanga's mistress Andrea Anders gave her great international exposure. She was to return to the Bond fold as Octopussy in 1983 (see pages 78 – 83).

Appearing briefly in the role of Saida the belly dancer was Carmen de Sautoy, who, since appearing in the Bond movie, developed into a serious dramatic actress. She is a member of the Royal Shakespeare Company and her TV credits include the Channel 4 film *Praying Mantis* and LWT's *Poirot*.

ABOVE: *(left) The Swedes who loved me: Maud Adams and Britt Ekland made a stunning Scandinavian duo in the ninth 007 movie. (right) Mary Goodnight (Britt Ekland) is wined and dined on Scaramanga's island.*

ABOVE: *Maud Adams relaxes during the hectic location shooting in Thailand.*

JAMES BOND averts Armageddon when he battles undersea villain Karl Stromberg. With the disappearance of nuclear submarines HMS *Ranger* and *Potemkin*, both the British and Russian Secret Services assign their best agents to investigate. Russian KGB General Gogol contacts their top operative agent Triple X (XXX), Major Anya Amasova, and orders her to report at once. Meanwhile, inside a log cabin somewhere in the Austrian Alps, James Bond is sharing an intimate moment with a beautiful blonde, when a ticker-tape message from M tells him to pull out immediately. The girl urges Bond to stay: 'But, James, I need you,' 'So does England,' comes the loyal reply. The girl radios a KGB death squad that Bond has just left but, using his acrobatic skills, he evades the Russian gunmen, killing their leader in the process.

Anya reports to General Gogol and he tells her there is a lead to follow up in Cairo. Before she leaves he tells her of the unfortunate death of her lover, Sergei, at the hands of the

The Spy Who Loved Me (1977)

JAMES BOND	ROGER MOORE
MAJOR ANYA AMASOVA	BARBARA BACH
STROMBERG	CURT JURGENS
JAWS	RICHARD KIEL
NAOMI	CAROLINE MUNRO
GENERAL GOGOL	WALTER GOTELL
MINISTER OF DEFENCE	GEOFFREY KEEN
M	BERNARD LEE
Q	DESMOND LLEWELYN
MISS MONEYPENNY	LOIS MAXWELL
PRODUCER	ALBERT R. BROCCOLI
DIRECTOR	LEWIS GILBERT
SCREENPLAY	CHRISTOPHER WOOD
	RICHARD MAIBAUM
PRODUCTION DESIGNER	KEN ADAM
DIRECTOR OF PHOTOGRAPHY	CLAUDE RENOIR

ABOVE: *(left) Even in the heat of the Egyptian desert, Bond (Roger Moore) and Anya (Barbara Bach) still look cool. (right) Beauty and the Beast: Anya and the menacing Jaws (Richard Kiel).*

British Secret Service. Meanwhile, Commander James Bond flies to Faslane Submarine Base in Scotland for a briefing with Admiral Hargreaves. It appears that someone has developed a way of recognizing the wake of a submarine underwater and is trying to sell the microfilmed plans on the black market.

In Atlantis, the underwater marine laboratory of Karl Stromberg off the coast of Sardinia, a transaction is taking place. Stromberg is about to pay Dr Bechmann and Professor Markovitz a vast sum of money for designing the submarine-tracking system. Then Stromberg's mood changes as he explains that he has discovered someone has been trying to sell copies of the plans to opposing world powers. Asking his female assistant to leave the room before he discusses the

Hosein, a Cambridge-educated Arab and old school friend of agent 007. Hosein tells Bond that he must reach club owner Max Kalba through a contact called Aziz Fekkesh if he wants to bid for the sale of the microfilm. Accepting the hospitality of his friend's harem Bond stays the night saying, 'When one is in Egypt one should delve deeply into its treasures!'

The following morning Bond visits Fekkesh's house to find he has left Felicca to keep him occupied. But Felicca is killed when she stops a bullet from Sandor's gun meant for Bond. 007 pushes the gunman off the roof – though not before he has told Bond where to find Fekkesh. That evening Bond arrives at the Great Pyramids of Giza and observes Fekkesh talking with Anya. When Fekkesh sees Jaws lurking in the

matter, Stromberg waits for her to enter the elevator. As the door closes she falls through a trapdoor into a tank, where she is devoured by a shark. So perishes anyone who would pervert Stromberg's goals for their own ends. The marine laboratory rises from the ocean bed and Stromberg calls for his two hired killers. Alone with the bulky Sandor and the seven-foot giant Jaws, he tells them that anyone who has come into contact with the microfilm tracking system is to be eliminated. A helicopter with the two scientists takes off from the laboratory launch pad and explodes. Stromberg picks up the telephone. 'Cancel the transfer for $20 million,' comes the cold-blooded instruction.

Bond travels by camel to Cairo via a Bedouin encampment in the desert. Entering a huge tent, Bond discovers a harem of Arab beauties administering to the every whim of

shadows, he panics and tries to run away – but Jaws catches up with the terrified man in a nearby tomb and kills him with his metal teeth. Bond discovers an appointment in the dead man's diary. Leaving the tomb, Bond is confronted by Anya, who asks him where Fekkesh is. 'With the pharaohs,' Bond tells her as he is set upon by Ivan and Boris, her two strongarm men. Knocking both men unconscious, 007 wishes Anya good night, hoping she has enjoyed the 'show'.

Bond meets Anya once again while visiting the Mujaba Club and informs her that he knows she is agent XXX. Bond approaches Kalba to bid for the microfilm but is opposed by Anya, who also wishes to place a bid. Kalba makes the keen observation, 'I see you have competition, Mr Bond, and from where I sit, I fancy you will find the lady's figure hard to match!'

ABOVE: *Major Anya Amasova – Agent Triple X – looks dressed to kill in everything she wears: (left) KGB uniform, (middle) Royal Navy Air Sea Rescue and (right) evening dress.*

ABOVE: *Shot on location in Sardinia, Caroline Munro shows why she remains one of the most popular Bond pin-up girls.*

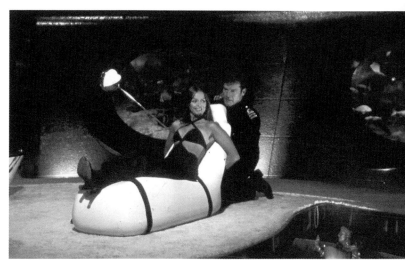

Stromberg's beautiful assistant, Naomi, and taken to Atlantis. Posing as Robert Sterling, a marine biologist, Bond is tested by the suspicious Stromberg on his knowledge of marine life. Later, Jaws confirms that Bond and Anya are the two agents he had dealt with earlier and Stromberg gives orders they should

Kalba is called away to the telephone by a hoax and killed by Jaws. Bond leaves an 'out of order' sign on the body, and leaps through an open window into Jaw's moving van, only to be joined by Anya. She asks what happened to Kalba, and Bond tells her, 'He was cut off – permanently.' Unbeknown to both Bond and Anya, Jaws is listening to their conversation from a speaker in the driver's seat. Arriving at the ancient temple ruins in the desert, Jaws attacks Bond. Then, pointing a gun at him, Anya forces Jaws to give her the microfilm, which he throws on the sand. When she kneels down to pick it up, Jaws sees his chance and kicks the gun out of her hand. He takes a swing at Bond and knocks the surrounding scaffolding down on top of himself. 'Egyptian builders,' quips Bond. Anya tries to start the van and leave Bond behind – but he has the keys. They race off together as Jaws reappears and systematically pulls the van to pieces.

Travelling down the Nile on an Arab dhow Anya gasses Bond and escapes with the microfilm, but not before Bond has examined the contents. Bond discovers M, Moneypenny, Gogol and Anya using a tomb as their joint headquarters. The rival governments have decided to pool their resources in an attempt to find the missing submarines. 'We have entered a new era of Anglo-Soviet cooperation,' says Gogol, but Bond realizes that vital technical details have been deleted from the photographed plans. On the train journey to Stromberg's ocean laboratory, Bond and Anya are once more attacked by Jaws, but 007 kicks him out of the carriage window.

Bond and Anya are met in Sardinia by Q with Bond's new Lotus Esprit. From their hotel they are collected by

be killed as soon as they get ashore. Sure enough, as they drive along a mountain road, Bond and Anya are attacked by a motorcyclist who fires his explosive sidecar at them. Avoiding the sidecar, Bond cuts in front of a truck carrying feather mattresses. The sidecar explodes on contact with the truck and the road is showered with millions of feathers. Unable to see where he is going, the motorcyclist rides over the edge of a cliff. 'All those feathers and he still can't fly.' Escaping a further attack from Jaws and his henchmen, Bond then takes to the water in his submersible car when machine-gunned by Naomi from her helicopter. Anya presses a button on the car's

ABOVE: *(left) Caroline Munro as Naomi, Stromberg's murderous helicopter pilot.*
(right) Bond rescues Anya from Stromberg's clutches, and later opens a bottle of bubbly to break the ice.

the Russian, American and British crews crowd into the last remaining submarine. Blasting their way through the bow doors, they escape as the giant tanker sinks beneath the waves.

Bond rides to Atlantis on a wetbike to rescue Anya before the submarine has to open fire on Stromberg's headquarters. Confronting Stromberg in his state room, Bond avoids an explosive harpoon and shoots him dead. 'You've shot your last bolt, Stromberg.' Cutting Anya free, they leave Atlantis in a jettisoned escape pod as the first torpedo hits its mark, but not before Bond has fought Jaws one last time. Bond uses a giant magnet to catch Jaws by the teeth and drops him into the shark pool, where the seven-foot giant succeeds in killing his fishy adversary and swimming away to safety. Reaching the surface in their pod, Anya points Bond's own gun at him, telling him the mission is over – but she cannot kill him. She falls into his arms instead.

Rescued by the Royal Navy, Bond and Anya are cuddling together under silk sheets, to the outrage of M, Q and Gogol. When the Minister of Defence asks, 'Bond, what do you think you're doing?' he replies, 'Keeping the British end up, sir!'

dashboard and a missile immediately shoots from the car blowing Naomi out of the sky.

Whilst investigating Atlantis in the submersible car, Bond and Anya are attacked by frogmen in armed underwater craft. Bond successfully disposes of the enemy but has to make for dry land as his car is taking in water. He drives out of the surf to the amazement of the holidaymakers on the beach, and winds down the window to eject a fish. Back at their hotel, Anya discovers Bond is responsible for the death of her lover and swears to kill 007 when their mission is over.

Bond and Anya are taken aboard the USS *Wayne*. Stromberg's supertanker, the *Liparus*, swallows the submarine and the crew are taken captive. Bond and Anya are brought before Stromberg, who plans to destroy New York and Moscow with missiles from the captured submarines – global destruction will follow, he assures them. He will then build a new undersea world of which he will be ruler. Stromberg orders his guards to imprison Bond with the rest of the naval personnel and departs for Atlantis taking Anya with him. Bond kills the guards and breaks the naval crews out of the brig. Battle rages inside the hull of the *Liparus*, and Bond uses an atomic detonator to gain entry to the near-impregnable control room. Once inside, he changes the coordinates of the missiles on the renegade submarines so they destroy each other. With the *Liparus* exploding around them, Bond and

ABOVE: *(left) It's amazing what you can pick up in the January sales! More over-the-top publicity shoot fun for Barbara and Richard. (right) While in Cairo, 007 is pleasantly distracted by Felicca (Olga Bisera).*

over 300 TV commercials and her other roles include a BBC TV production of *Dracula* with Louis Jourdan.

Yugoslav actress Olga Bisera, who portrayed the ill-fated Felicca, retired from acting, married, and became a journalist and prolific author.

MAJOR ANYA AMASOVA as portrayed by American actress Barbara Bach was the first Bond girl who was the equal of Bond in every way. The two characters spend the majority of the story trying to score points against each other – and she gives Bond a good run for his money. A top model at the age of 17, Barbara's 5ft 7in 35-24-35 figure was destined to grace the covers of major magazines around the world. She worked for the famed Eileen Ford Agency and it was while she was on an assignment in Rome for *Seventeen* magazine that she fell in love with Italy and a young Italian industrialist. She appeared in several Italian films before appearing in *The Spy Who Loved Me*. She is now married to ex-Beatle Ringo Starr. Her other screen appearances include *Force 10 from Navarone* (1978), *The Humanoid* (1978) and *Caveman* (1981).

Stromberg's helicopter pilot Naomi, Caroline Munro, has adorned many calendars in her career as a photographic model. She occasionally appears on TV game shows and has appeared in films including *The Abominable Dr. Phibes* (1971), *Dracula A.D. 1972* (1972), *The Golden Voyage of Sinbad* (1973) and *At The Earth's Core* (1976).

Bond has his hands full in the Austrian log cabin sequence with British girl Sue Vanner. Sue has appeared in

ABOVE: *(top) 'I need you, James' from Sue Vanner wrapped in fur just isn't enough to keep our man Bond tucked up by the fireside – England needs him! (middle) 'The gentleman will have a Martini, shaken not stirred.' Anya and Bond play at one-upmanship. (bottom) On the sea voyage to Atlantis, only Anya was sensible enough to wear a crocheted hat.*

Moonraker (1979)

JAMES BOND	ROGER MOORE
HOLLY GOODHEAD	LOIS CHILES
DRAX	MICHAEL LONSDALE
JAWS	RICHARD KIEL
CORINNE DUFOUR	CORINNE CLERY
M	BERNARD LEE
FREDERICK GRAY	GEOFFREY KEEN
Q	DESMOND LLEWELYN
MANUELA	EMILY BOLTON
MISS MONEYPENNY	LOIS MAXWELL
PRODUCER	ALBERT R. BROCCOLI
DIRECTOR	LEWIS GILBERT
SCREENPLAY	CHRISTOPHER WOOD
PRODUCTION DESIGNER	KEN ADAM
DIRECTOR OF PHOTOGRAPHY	JEAN TOURNIER

JAMES BOND is pitted against Hugo Drax and his diabolical scheme to repopulate the world with a race of perfect physical specimens.

An RAF Boeing 747 is carrying a Moonraker space shuttle on loan from the US government when it launches from the back of the 747, destroying the aircraft. Bond is briefed on the disappearance of the Moonraker on his return from an assignment in Africa, where he narrowly escapes death at the hands of Jaws. Before Bond sets off on his mission to find the missing space shuttle, Q equips him with a deadly dart-firing wristwatch. 'Very novel, Q, you must get them in the stores for Christmas,' suggests 007.

Bond is collected in California by Drax's personal pilot, Corinne Dufour, on the first stage of his mission. They fly over the Moonraker complex, and in the distance Bond is amazed to see Drax's home – a magnificent French château built in the desert. He has had it shipped over and re-built brick by brick. When Bond visits Drax in his palatial drawingroom, he is under the misapprehension that Bond has come to apologize on behalf of the British government for the loss of his space shuttle. Paraphrasing Oscar Wilde, Drax goes on, 'To lose one aircraft may be regarded as a misfortune. To lose two seems like carelessness.' As Bond leaves, Drax tells his bodyguard, Chang, 'Look after Mr Bond – see that some harm comes to him.'

Corinne takes Bond to meet Dr Holly Goodhead. 'You're a woman,' says a surprised Bond. 'Your powers of observation do you credit, Mr Bond,' says Holly. She invites

ABOVE: *(left) 007 (Roger Moore) discovers that Holly Goodhead (Lois Chiles) is also a CIA agent.*
(right) Dr Goodhead, an astrophysicist at Drax's desert complex.
RIGHT: *Holly Goodhead is the most qualified of all the Bond Girls, an astrophysicist, NASA astronaut and CIA operative.*

Bond to try the centrifuge – a revolving arm which is used to simulate the gravity force experienced when an astronaut is shot into space. Bond asks how fast it will go. Holly explains that 3g is equivalent to take-off pressure and most people pass out at 7. Holly is called away to the telephone by Drax as Bond's ride begins. In the control room, Chang increases the speed to 13g but Bond disables the controls with an explosive dart from his wristwatch. Understandably reluctant to accept a helping hand from Holly, Bond stumbles dizzily from the cockpit. Recovering his balance, he notices Chang leaving the control room.

That night Bond visits Corinne's room and learns more about Drax. Corinne tells him that her mother gave her a list of things not to do on a first date. 'That's not what I came for,' says 007. 'No,' says Corinne, rather surprised. Bond learns that Drax has been working on something very secret, but it has been moved. Sitting on the bed, Bond kisses Corinne. 'What about that list of your mother's?' asks Bond. 'I never learned to read,' she replies invitingly. Leaving Corinne asleep, Bond decides to investigate Drax's study. He opens the safe and is photographing some documents when he is interrupted by Corinne. Unbeknown to either of them, their intrusion has been watched by Chang.

The next morning Bond leaves Drax's estate, but not before he despatches a game warden instructed by Drax to kill him. Later, Corinne is summoned by Drax. Her employment is terminated immediately when Chang sets Drax's Dobermann guard dogs on her.

Bond discovers from the photographed documents that a glass factory in Venice is manufacturing top-secret components for the Drax Corporation. Arriving in St Mark's Square, 007 determines to investigate the Venini glass factory and asks the receptionist if he may join the visitors' guided tour of the museum. Once inside he notices Holly is a member of the party. He follows her outside and asks her to join him for dinner that evening, but she refuses. During the day, 007 has to deal with a knife-throwing 'corpse' and water-borne gunmen, but he returns to the glass factory later that evening. In a glass-walled laboratory technicians are placing phials containing liquid into strange globes. Bond is about to investigate the contents of the phials but is disturbed by the returning technicians. Hurriedly placing a phial in his pocket, he leaves another lying carelessly on a globe as he goes out of the lab. As the technicians move the globe, they dislodge the phial and it falls to the floor, spilling its contents. Bond watches, horrified, as the two men die instantly. Chang attacks Bond as he returns through the glass museum. In a fight which demolishes the priceless contents of the museum, Bond eventually throws Chang to his death through a giant clock face.

Confronting Holly in her hotel bedroom, Bond discovers she is in fact a CIA agent and, seeing an ice bucket containing champagne, he remarks, 'Bollinger. If it's '69 you

ABOVE: *(top) Jaws (Richard Kiel) finds true love in space with the diminutive Dolly (Blanche Ravalec).*
(bottom) While in Brazil, 007 finds time to dally with Manuela (Emily Bolton).

Back on firm ground, Bond notices a lovely girl beckoning him. He follows her through the jungle into the ruins of a Mayan temple and is greeted by yet more beautiful girls – when Drax makes his entrance. Long-term exposure to the orchid causes infertility, he explains, but he has improved on this and its seeds now yield death. Holly is also held prisoner at the temple and together they are placed in a room directly beneath the Moonraker's exhausts. They escape from threatened incineration, steal a Moonraker and follow Drax and his other shuttles to their rendezvous in space. To their amazement, Drax has built a space station, undetectable on the radar screen. The

were expecting me.' The two agents decide to pool their resources. M and the Minister of Defence join Bond to investigate the glass factory and the whole party dons gas masks. However, the laboratory has been moved and in its place stands a palatial office where Drax is at work. 'Excuse me, gentlemen, but not being English I sometimes find your sense of humour rather difficult to follow,' says Drax, mocking the intruders. Meanwhile, with the death of Chang, Drax is in need of a new bodyguard and hires Jaws.

Landing in Rio, Bond meets his contact, Manuela. He explains to her he wants to visit Drax's warehouse that night. 'How do you kill five hours in Rio if you don't samba?' asks Bond, loosening Manuela's robe. That night Bond and Manuela fight their way through carnival-packed streets to the warehouse. It appears to be empty but 007 finds a packing label marked 'Drax Air Freight'. Manuela is attacked by Jaws but he is dragged off by a party of carnival revellers. Holly arrives in Rio and she and Bond board a cable car to investigate 'Drax Air Freight', but as the cable car begins its ascent, Jaws jams the drive wheel. He climbs up the cable and on to the car. After a struggle, Bond pushes Jaws through the cable-car roof, and he and Holly slide down the cable on a chain. Jaws crashes into the control station and, climbing from the wreckage, he is assisted by the diminutive Dolly. Affectionately, they walk away holding hands.

Bond has escaped the clutches of Drax's thugs, but Holly has been taken prisoner. Riding to Q's workshop on the pampas, Bond learns the phials from Drax's laboratory contained a nerve gas, highly toxic for humans but harmless to animals. The chemical formula has been derived from a rare orchid, so Bond travels by boat to where the plant was last reported seen. However, Jaws is also in the upper regions of the Tipperapi River and he leads an armed attack on 007's craft. As they approach a large waterfall Bond escapes on a hang-glider, destroying his pursuers. Jaws crashes over the falls.

Moonrakers dock at the space station and the two agents go aboard to disable the radar-jamming system. At the same time as the first globe of nerve gas is released, both agents are captured by Jaws. Drax compares Bond's presence on the station with 'the tedious inevitability of an unloved season.'

The tension mounts as globe number two is launched and the laser is activated to destroy an American intercepting shuttle. Drax is about to have Bond and Holly expelled through the air lock, but Bond points out to Jaws that he and Dolly will not be included in Drax's rebirth of the Earth. Furious, Jaws joins forces with the two agents to destroy the

ABOVE: *(left) Delivering women by the truckload – it could only happen in a James Bond movie. (right) Bond is escorted to an audience with Drax by Corinne Dufour (Corinne Clery), his personal helicopter pilot.*

ABOVE: *Corinne Clery is undoubtedly one of the sexiest actresses ever to appear in the Bond series.*

atmosphere the Moonraker begins to overheat and the automatic laser malfunctions. Bond switches to manual and destroys the last globe just as it is entering the Earth's atmosphere. Coming into range of an American tracking ship, the image of Bond and Holly floating in zero gravity, naked but for a sheet, is beamed from the remote on board TV monitors. Watched with shock and surprise by M, Q and the Minister of Defence, the minister asks, 'My God, what's Bond doing?' 'I think he's attempting re-entry,' replies a bemused Q. Seeing the TV camera, Bond smiles and switches it off as Holly murmurs, 'Take me round the world one more time, James!'

HOLLY GOODHEAD is the most qualified of all the Bond Girls, an astrophysicist, NASA astronaut and CIA operative.

space station and a 'laser battle' breaks out as American spacetroopers infiltrate the headquarters. Bond shoots Drax with a poisonous dart from his watch and, inviting him to 'take a giant leap for mankind', ejects him into space. Jaws and Dolly are rescued by the American shuttle and Bond and Holly chase after the deadly globes in the last remaining Moonraker.

Bond destroys globes two and three in time but the first one launched proves more of a problem. Skirting the Earth's

She is also Bond's equal in unarmed combat, and single-handedly despatches two of Drax's guards. Texan actress Lois Chiles won the role after sitting next to director Lewis Gilbert on a plane. Later he remembered her and asked Cubby Broccoli what he thought and he agreed she would be excellent. Starting her career as a model, she once posed for the cover of *Elle* magazine. Her other appearances include *The Great Gatsby* (1974), *Death on the Nile* (1978) and *Creepshow 2* (1988). She also appeared in TV's *Dallas* opposing the all-powerful J. R. Ewing.

Parisian Corinne Clery featured as Corinne Dufour, the unfortunate victim of Drax's killer dogs. Miss Clery first came to prominence in the controversial film *The Story of O* (1975) and also appeared in *The Humanoid* (1978) with Barbara Bach and Richard Kiel. She has a son by her first marriage.

ABOVE: *(top) Captured by Jaws, Holly and Bond are brought before celestial megalomaniac Hugo Drax.*
(middle) Mellow yellow! Lois Chiles and Roger Moore pose in their Drax Industries space gear.
(right) All done by wires! Bond and Holly appear to defy gravity inside Drax's space station.

For Your Eyes Only (1981)

JAMES BOND	ROGER MOORE
MELINA	CAROLE BOUQUET
COLUMBO	TOPOL
BIBI	LYNN-HOLLY JOHNSON
KRISTATOS	JULIAN GLOVER
LISL	CASSANDRA HARRIS
BRINK	JILL BENNETT
LOCQUE	MICHAEL GOTHARD
HAVELOCK	JACK HEDLEY
GENERAL GOGOL	WALTER GOTELL
MISS MONEYPENNY	LOIS MAXWELL
Q	DESMOND LLEWELYN
PRODUCER	ALBERT R. BROCCOLI
EXECUTIVE PRODUCER	MICHAEL G. WILSON
DIRECTOR	JOHN GLEN
SCREENPLAY	RICHARD MAIBAUM
	MICHAEL G. WILSON
DIRECTOR OF PHOTOGRAPHY	ALAN HUME
PRODUCTION DESIGNER	PETER LAMONT

JAMES BOND races against time to recover a top-secret tracking system before it falls into the hands of Russian agents.

On a visit to the grave of his late wife, James Bond survives an attempt on his life by wheelchair-bound Blofeld and despatches the villain down a nearby chimney stack. Meanwhile, off the Albanian coast, the British spyship the *St Georges* sinks with all hands after it strikes a floating World War II mine. Unfortunately, the sea in that area is too shallow to ensure that the secret British tracking device remains undiscovered by a foreign power. The Russians have already contacted their usual 'friend' in Greece to look into it should the device come on the market.

Returning by seaplane from a shopping spree in Athens, Melina Havelock is greeted by her parents on board their research vessel the *Triana*. Suddenly the seaplane returns and strafes the deck with machine-gun fire, killing Melina's parents.

Meanwhile, at the headquarters of the British Secret Service, agent 007 is assigned to recover the missing ATAC – Automatic Targeting Attack Communicator. The machine is used as an ultra-low-frequency coded transmitter to launch British submarine ballistic missiles. If the transmitter were to fall into the hands of the enemy, it would mean every order could be countermanded – or worse, British submarines could be ordered to attack their own cities. Bond must find Hector Gonzales, the pilot who murdered the Havelocks, and apply whatever pressure is necessary to discover who hired him.

ABOVE: *(left) Melina Havelock (Carole Bouquet) joins Columbo and his men in the assault on Kristatos's mountain-top hideaway. (right) 007's object of desire: Carole Bouquet.*

Bond investigates the hit man's villa in Spain but is captured by his guards. Gonzales orders him taken away to be killed when he recognizes Bond as an intelligence agent, but Gonzales is perforated by a crossbow bolt as he dives into his swimming pool. Bond uses the diversion to escape and catches the owner of the crossbow – the Havelock's daughter, Melina. Safe in Melina's hotel room, Bond advises her to forget her quest for vengeance, telling her, 'The Chinese have a saying: "Before setting out on revenge you first dig two graves."' Melina is unimpressed, 'I don't expect *you* to understand, but I'm half Greek – and Greek women, like Electra, always avenge their loved ones!'

Bond tracks down Emile Locque, the pay-off man at Gonzales's villa, to Cortina, where the man is working for

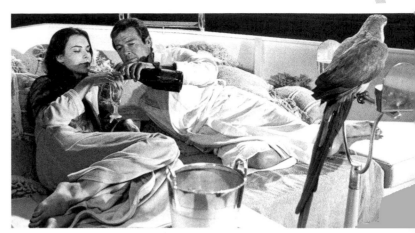

ABOVE: *(top) Bond (Roger Moore) and Melina celebrate the end of a successful mission.*
(bottom) Melina 'perforates' the murderer of her parents.

Bond, skiing back to his hotel, is ambushed by Kreigler and then chased by the two motorcyclists. He escapes the clutches of his pursuers and drives to the indoor ice rink with Ferrara. Before he leaves he is attacked by three hockey players. Bond wins three-nil. Back at his car he finds Ferrara, murdered, and clutching a dove emblem.

Bond travels to Corfu and, dining with Kristatos at a local casino, they witness a 'scene' between Countess Lisl and Columbo. As the Countess leaves, it is apparent that she wants Bond to follow. Although it could be a trap, Bond escorts Lisl to her beach-house. The following morning Bond and Lisl are strolling along the beach when they are surprised by Locque and his man Claus in beach buggies. Lisl is run down and killed by Locque, and Claus holds 007 at gunpoint. But Claus is himself killed by a group of men wearing wet suits bearing the dove emblem. Bending over Lisl's body, Bond is knocked unconscious. When he regains consciousness he is aboard ship. He is taken to Columbo's cabin and the smuggler explains that it is Kristatos he wants, and Locque is *his* man. 'Why should I believe you?' asks 007. 'I'll prove it to you!' promises Columbo, returning Bond's PPK. 'Tonight we'll go together to his warehouse in Albania.' Columbo then goes on to explain that Kristatos worked as a double agent during the fighting in Crete in World War II, and now works for the Russians against both their countries.

Bond and Columbo's men sail to the wharf and attack the warehouse but Locque detonates a bomb, destroying the building. His attempt to escape up a tunnelled mountain road

Greek smugglers. Bond's contact, Ferrara, introduces him to Anglophile Ari Kristatos, who is watching his protégée, ice-skater Bibi Dahl, go through her paces. He tells Bond that Locque is the right-hand man of Columbo – a smuggler, white slaver and specialist in contract murder, known in the Greek underworld as 'the Dove'. On the way to his hotel Bond is just in time to save Melina from the murderous intentions of two black-suited motorcyclists. He tells her it will be safer for her to go back to the *Triana*. Returning to his hotel, Bond is astounded to find Bibi waiting for him in his bed. Bond tells her to get her clothes on and he will buy her an ice-cream. He escorts Bibi to the biathlon, where they watch another of her 'conquests', Eric Kreigler, take part.

ABOVE: *(left) Baby Doll! Lynn-Holly Johnson as the man-hungry ice-skating prodigy Bibi Dahl.*
(right) Bibi throws herself at Bond (Roger Moore), who offers to buy her an ice-cream.

is cut off when he is wounded by Bond. His car swerves off the road to hang precariously on the cliff edge. Bond approaches Locque holding a dove badge. 'You left this with Ferrara,' says a grim-faced 007. Tossing the badge to Locque, Bond kicks the car over the cliff edge. 'He had no head for heights!'

Bond swims to meet Melina on the ocean floor, where they leave her air tank. They decide to investigate the wreck of the *St Georges* in the two-man submarine, *Neptune*, and discover the ATAC to be undamaged. They are attacked by a man in a diving suit whom Bond despatches with the aid of the explosive timer from the attack communicator. However, in their absence, the *Triana* has been overrun by Kristatos and his men and he is intent on having some sport with his captives. Hoping to attract sharks, Kristatos has Bond and Melina tied together and dragged over the razor-sharp coral. The captives dive deep, and 007 lashes the rope around a large piece of coral. Kristatos's boat strains and the rope snaps. Bond and Melina hide on the sea bed, breathing from her air tank, until Kristatos believes them devoured by sharks.

Bond discovers the ATAC has been taken to St Cyril's. Enlisting the assistance of Columbo and his men, 007 prepares to make a back-breaking climb to the deserted monastery which Kristatos is using as a hideout. After killing a guard who succeeds in 'getting the drop' on him, Bond winches Melina, Columbo and his men up to the monastery. Bond and Columbo surprise the guards and, in the ensuing fight, Bond crashes through a window, taking the guard with him, only to be confronted by the imposing figure of Eric Kreigler. 007 is saved by Bibi when she hangs on to Kreigler's gun-arm, but is slapped to the ground by the big man. Bond is on the receiving end of some hefty punches from the KGB strongarm man, when Kristatos, retreating to safety with the ATAC, distracts Kreigler and Bond pushes him through a window to his death. Columbo engages Kristatos in a desperate struggle, and the ATAC falls to the ground, to be picked up by Bond. Reminding Melina about 'those two graves', Bond prevents her from killing Kristatos, who, unnoticed by 007, has pulled a stiletto. Just in time, Columbo's knife thuds into his back. General Gogol arrives by helicopter to purchase the attack communicator. As Gogol approaches, Bond throws the ATAC over the cliff. 'That's détente, comrade. You don't have it, I don't have it,' smiles Bond.

Returning to the *Triana*, Bond and Melina swim naked in the moonlight.

'DON'T TELL *me* what to do!' says Melina Havelock to James Bond, a liberated woman with a doctorate in marine archaeology. Born in 1957, French actress Carole Bouquet was educated at a convent school. She studied briefly at the Sorbonne, but decided to try acting, and attended the National School of Theatre at the Paris Conservatoire. She left the Conservatoire for the starring role in Luis Buñuel's

ABOVE: *007's liaison with Lisl (Cassandra Harris) is cut tragically short when the villainous Locque runs her down.*

That Obscure Object of Desire (1977). She won rave reviews on both sides of the Atlantic and the film was nominated for an Academy Award. Her other appearances include *Buffet Froid* (1979) [US title *Cold Cuts*]. She succeeded Catherine Deneuve – who once turned down the offer to appear as a Bond girl – as the Chanel girl.

Born on 13 December 1958 in Glenview, Chicago, Lynn-Holly Johnson always wanted to ice-skate and had an impressive career as an amateur ice figure-skater before turning professional when she joined the Ice Capades Show in 1977 as principal performer. The precocious man-eater Bibi Dahl was only her third screen role. Her other films include *Ice Castles* (1978) and *Watcher in the Woods* (1979).

Cassandra Harris played the part of Columbo's ill-fated mistress Lisl. In her native Australia she co-hosted her own live TV chatshow called *Beauty and the Beast*. She toured with the National Theatre and appeared in commercials and TV shows such as *Enemy at the Door*. Her other screen appearances include *The Greek Tycoon* (1978) and *Rough Cut* (1980). Wife of the fifth 007, actor Pierce Brosnan, she died of cancer in January 1992, the day after their eleventh wedding anniversary.

ABOVE: *Bond (Roger Moore) and Bibi (Lynn-Holly Johnson) watch her latest conquest,*
Kreigler, take part in the biathlon.

ABOVE: *(left) Melina (Carole Bouquet) and Bond (Roger Moore) about to become appetising shark bait.*
(right & bottom) For your eyes only! To date, Sheena Easton is the only title singer ever to appear in the opening
credits of a Bond movie; directed here by Maurice Binder, and lit by cameraman Arthur Wooster.

JAMES BOND uncovers a plot to detonate an atomic bomb on an American air base by a renegade Russian general and an ex-Afghan prince.

James Bond reports to the offices of the British Secret Service after successfully completing an assignment in South America with the sultry Bianca. Much to Moneypenny's annoyance, 007 hands a bunch of carnations to Penelope Smallbone, Moneypenny's young and beautiful new assistant. Agent 009 has been found dead in West Berlin clutching what appeared to be a priceless Fabergé egg. On closer inspection the ornamental egg is proved to be a fake. M tells Bond he is to accompany Jim Fanning – the Service's art expert – to Sotheby's, where an identical egg is being auctioned. The sale of the egg could be a covert operation by the Russians attempting to raise currency for payoffs. Bond and Fanning must try to identify the seller.

Meanwhile, at a high-ranking Russian disarmament meeting in the Kremlin, General Gogol is arguing against the

Octopussy (1983)

JAMES BOND	ROGER MOORE
OCTOPUSSY	MAUD ADAMS
KAMAL KHAN	LOUIS JOURDAN
MAGDA	KRISTINA WAYBORN
GOBINDA	KABIR BEDI
GENERAL ORLOV	STEVEN BERKOFF
Q	DESMOND LLEWELYN
M	ROBERT BROWN
MISS MONEYPENNY	LOIS MAXWELL
GOGOL	WALTER GOTELL
VIJAY	VIJAY AMRITRAJ
PRODUCER	ALBERT R. BROCCOLI
EXECUTIVE PRODUCER	MICHAEL G. WILSON
DIRECTOR	JOHN GLEN
SCREENPLAY	GEORGE MACDONALD FRASER
	RICHARD MAIBAUM
	MICHAEL G. WILSON
DIRECTOR OF PHOTOGRAPHY	ALAN HUME
PRODUCTION DESIGNER	PETER LAMONT

ABOVE: *(left) Octopussy (Maud Adams) and her all-girl fighting troupe.*
(right) KGB General Gogol's assistant Rubelvitch (Eva Rueber-Staier),
strikes a pose on Peter Lamont's impressive war room set.

ABOVE: *Octopussy displays why smuggling is a more lucrative profession than being a circus-owner.*

ABOVE: *The perfect takeaway! Kristina Wayborn as Octopussy's lieutenant, Magda.*

Octopussy,' replies Magda. Magda steals the egg from Bond's coat pocket and slides down from the balcony using her sari to be driven away in Khan's waiting car. Bond is knocked out by Gobinda and regains consciousness to find himself a prisoner at Khan's home – the Monsoon Palace. Using the acid from his pen, Bond escapes from his room, only to see a helicopter land carrying General Orlov. Homing in on the egg, Bond learns more of Khan and Orlov's plan but the homing device is revealed when, believing the egg that Khan has recovered to be the fake, Orlov smashes it. Bond's escape is discovered and Khan, Gobinda and a group of tribesmen track Bond through the jungle. Braving a tiger, leeches and crocodiles, Bond finally escapes on a tourist boat.

Bond learns from Q that Magda's tattoo is connected with a fabulously wealthy woman. She is known as Octopussy and lives in the Floating Palace with her female entourage. 'Sexual discrimination,' cries Bond, on learning that men are not allowed on Octopussy's island. 'I'll definitely have to pay a visit,' he says, raising an eyebrow. As good as his word, Bond steals into Octopussy's palace, unaware she is watching him on close-circuit TV. 'Am I to be your target for tonight?' asks Octopussy as Bond enters her quarters. Bond learns her nickname was given to her as a child by her father, not only an expert on octopuses, but a man Bond had been sent to arrest

folly of General Orlov's proposal to use armed aggression against NATO forces in Europe. Later, at the Kremlin Art Repository, Orlov learns that the fake egg has been stolen in transit – the genuine egg must be returned, whatever the cost.

At the auction, Bond and Fanning notice the arrival of a beautiful blonde who joins a dark man. Fanning tells Bond the man is 'Kamal Khan, usually a seller, marginal politician, dubious sources'. Khan opens the bidding for the egg and Bond bids against him to see how high the man will go. Khan raises his bid to half a million pounds and Bond has his answer. Bond, however, has switched the original egg for the fake. A legitimate buyer would complain at being sold a fake, but Khan – Bond thinks not!

Bond follows Khan to Delhi. Sadruddin, head of Station I, and his assistant Vijay meet 007 and Vijay later observes him engage Kamal Khan in a game of backgammon. Using the genuine egg as surety, Bond defeats Khan with his own weighted dice. Khan is not amused. 'Spend the money quickly, Mr Bond,' says Khan threateningly. Bond and Vijay are soon attacked by thugs led by Khan's bodyguard, Gobinda, and, escaping through a camouflaged billboard, they find themselves in Q's portable workshop. Q conceals a microphone homing device inside the Fabergé egg, and equips Bond with a pen that releases acid, and a radio-directional watch which will enable him to track the egg.

That evening Bond has dinner with Magda, Khan's blonde associate. The couple retire to Bond's bedroom, where, seeing a tattoo of an octopus on Magda's buttock, Bond asks, 'Forgive my curiosity, but what's that?' 'Oh, that's my little

ABOVE: *(left) Octopussy and her circus troupe are carried across Europe on their own train.*
(right) A girl of all trades! Magda also acts as ringmaster for Octopussy's circus,
while 007 (Roger Moore) masquerades as a knife-thrower.

many years ago. Octopussy became involved in smuggling when her father's old contacts approached her with a commission. Since then she has diversified into shipping, hotels, carnivals and circuses. Later that night, in bed, Bond and Octopussy are attacked by thugs hired by Khan. Although 007 successfully despatches the villains, he crashes through a window with the last surviving intruder. Allowing Octopussy to believe he has been killed by a crocodile, Bond returns to shore to hear the bad news – Vijay has been murdered by the thugs whilst on watch.

Octopussy's circus next appears in Karl Marx Stadt, so Bond travels to East Germany. Octopussy and Khan entertain Orlov but Bond overhears that Khan and Orlov plan to switch the last carriage of the travelling circus train without Octopussy's knowledge. She believes the circus cannon will contain a fortune in gems. It will in fact carry an atomic bomb. Bond is attacked by one of the twins in a deadly knife-throwing duo. Disposing of the twin, he is surprised by General Orlov. At gunpoint the General confesses that he intends to explode the bomb on an American air base, explaining there will be no fear of reprisals as everyone will assume it was an American bomb triggered accidentally. Europe will insist on unilateral disarmament and leave every border undefended for the Russians to walk across at will. They are disturbed when a Russian guard opens the carriage door. Bond shoots him dead but, seizing his chance, Orlov escapes. Bond steals Orlov's car and, with the tyres shredded by machine-gun bullets, Bond takes the car on to the rails and drives after the speeding train. The car is switched to the opposite side of the tracks and Bond jumps on to the circus train just as a train coming towards him smashes his car from the tracks. Meanwhile, Orlov has driven

to the border in an attempt to reach the train, but is shot by West German guards.

Bond – disguised in a gorilla suit – watches as Gobinda sets the bomb's timer. But Bond is discovered and a desperate struggle ensues on the roof of the train. The second twin in the deadly knife-throwing duo appears on the carriage roof. He and 007 fall from the speeding train and Bond kills him with one of his own knives. Disguising himself as a clown, Bond enters the big top to defuse the bomb. Unable to convince the base commander of the danger, 007 is restrained by security guards until Octopussy shoots the lock off the cannon to reveal the bomb countdown. Bond removes the detonator, only moments before the bomb is due to explode!

Khan has returned to India and Octopussy has followed him there. She confronts him but is overpowered by his guards as Magda and the island girls attack the Monsoon Palace. Bond arrives in a hot air balloon piloted by Q. Khan and Gobinda escape by horse, carrying an unconscious Octopussy to a waiting aircraft. Bond gallops after them and jumps on to the aircraft at the point of take-off. Khan takes the plane into a spin in order to dislodge 007, but to no avail. He then orders Gobinda to 'Go out there and get him!' But Bond dislodges Gobinda, who falls to his death. Forcing the tail ailerons down with his feet, Bond makes Khan bring the aircraft down on a small plateau as he and Octopussy jump from the hatch. Losing control of the aircraft, Khan plummets to his death over the edge of the plateau, crashing into the mountainside ahead.

'I wish you weren't in such a weakened condition,' says Octopussy as she and Bond relax on her barge. With that Bond relieves himself of both traction and bandages, undergoing a miraculous cure. 'Oh, James!' sighs Octopussy.

ABOVE: *Glamourpussy! (left) Bond is aided in his escape from a banana republic by the sultry Bianca (Tina Hudson). (right) Octopussy's all-woman army is staffed by muscular babes like Caroline Seward.*
OPPOSITE: *'Am I to be your target for tonight?' Octopussy inevitably falls for the devilish smooth charm of 007.*

MAUD ADAMS was the only actress ever to play two leading roles in a James Bond film, as well as playing the only female part to be featured as a title character in the series. A superb linguist, Maud speaks Swedish, French, German, Italian and English. She was born just below the Arctic Circle in Lulea, Sweden, on 12 February 1945. She gave up her modelling career in 1978 and decided to concentrate all her energies on acting. Her other movie appearances include *The Hostage Tower* (1980) and *Tattoo* (1980). She also appeared with Vanessa Redgrave in the TV film *Playing for Time*, and starred regularly in the series *Chicago Story*.

Octopussy's right-hand girl, Magda, was another character well able to handle herself in tricky situations, and the natural athleticism of Swedish actress Kristina Wayborn was ideally suited for the role. Born on a small island in the Baltic Sea, Kristina became a Swedish track champion, and can run 100 metres in 11.3 seconds. It's a wonder that James Bond caught her at all. Kristina has had an interesting and varied career as a racing driver, a jockey and horse trainer, a wild animal trainer and clothes designer. She trained with the famous director Ingmar Bergman for three years at the Royal Academy of Stockholm, and worked under a five-year contract modelling for Fabergé until being chosen by David Wolper to play Greta Garbo in the TV mini-series *Movieola*.

Gogol's assistant Rubelvitch was portrayed by 1969 ex-Miss World Eva Rueber-Staier. She first appeared as the character in *The Spy Who Loved Me* (1977) and returned as the same character for two more outings in *For Your Eyes Only* (1981) and *Octopussy* (1983). Austrian born, Eva's other credits include *Carry On Dick* (1974) and *Royal Flash* (1975).

A View To A Kill (1985)

JAMES BOND	ROGER MOORE
MAX ZORIN	CHRISTOPHER WALKEN
STACEY SUTTON	TANYA ROBERTS
MAY DAY	GRACE JONES
TIBBETT	PATRICK MACNEE
SCARPINE	PATRICK BAUCHAU
CHUCK LEE	DAVID YIP
POLA IVANOVA	FIONA FULLERTON
JENNY FLEX	ALISON DOODY
Q	DESMOND LLEWELYN
M	ROBERT BROWN
MISS MONEYPENNY	LOIS MAXWELL
GENERAL GOGOL	WALTER GOTELL
PRODUCERS	ALBERT R. BROCCOLI
	MICHAEL G. WILSON
DIRECTOR	JOHN GLEN
SCREENPLAY	RICHARD MAIBAUM
	MICHAEL G. WILSON
PRODUCTION DESIGNER	PETER LAMONT
DIRECTOR OF PHOTOGRAPHY	ALAN HUME

JAMES BOND battles against the prodigy of Nazi experimentation and his attempt to corner the world market in microchips.

James Bond is in Siberia, recovering a microchip from the body of 003, when he has to evade Russian ski troops and escape in an 'iceberg craft' piloted by agent Kimberley Jones. 'Oh, Commander Bond,' she says as he unzips her jumpsuit. 'Call me James – it's five days to Alaska,' replies Bond suavely. Bond discovers from Q that the microchip taken from the Russian research establishment is identical to the one developed by Zorin Industries. Before this development, all microchips had been susceptible to damage from the intense magnetic pulse of a nuclear explosion. One burst in outer space over the UK and everything with a microchip in it from the modern toaster to the most sophisticated computers – not to mention British defence systems – would be rendered absolutely useless. Realizing that the Russians must have a mole in Zorin's research company Bond is ordered to make discreet enquiries.

At Royal Ascot Bond meets Sir Godfrey Tibbett, who is attached to the Service. Tibbett 'smells a rat' when Zorin's horse Pegasus wins its race, as its lineage is poor. In the winner's enclosure, Zorin, and his striking girl companion, May Day, are pointed out to Bond. Tibbett explains that a friend of his, a French private detective, is investigating Zorin's background and Bond should travel to Paris to learn of his progress.

Bond meets Monsieur Aubergine in the restaurant at the Eiffel Tower but the detective is killed before he can pass on all he has learned. The black-suited killer eludes 007, jumping from the tower and parachuting to a waiting speedboat. The killer was May Day, assisted by Zorin at the wheel of the speedboat.

Posing as James St John-Smythe and with Tibbett as his chauffeur, Bond is driven to Zorin's stud farm to attend his thoroughbred sale. Bond is greeted by Pan-Ho, an Oriental girl, and Scarpine, Zorin's security chief. Bond is escorted to his room in the château by Jenny Flex – leaving Tibbett to struggle with the luggage. A helicopter lands and Bond and Tibbett watch as Zorin greets its passenger – a glamorous blonde girl. That evening at a reception for the buyers Bond notices Zorin writing a cheque for his blonde visitor. Investigating Zorin's desk, he discovers the cheque was for five million dollars and made payable to S. Sutton. Mingling with the guests, Bond photographs Dr Carl Mortner and oilman Bob Conley with his camera ring. Zorin introduces himself to Bond but is soon called away. When Bond begins talking to Miss Sutton, Zorin sends May Day to break up their conversation. May Day tells Zorin she is sure she has seen St John-Smythe somewhere before.

That night Bond and Tibbett investigate Pegasus's stable and discover that his stall is an elevator, descending to a basement laboratory. Using a stethoscope, Bond cracks the safe, while Tibbett discovers that Pegasus has recently undergone surgery. An electronically operated hypodermic

ABOVE: *Bond (Roger Moore) and Stacey Sutton (Tanya Roberts) watch as Zorin loses his grip – quite a problem when hanging from the Golden Gate bridge.*
OPPOSITE: *Wacky races! Only the fabulous Grace Jones as May Day could wear an outfit like this at Ascot and carry it off!*

needle suggests that Dr Mortner has implanted a microchip into the horse. The microchip, programmed to control an injection of additional horse steroids to overcome fatigue during a race, could be triggered by a remote-control transmitter small enough to fit into the tip of a jockey's whip. Two guards notice that the stall has descended into the basement and investigate. Hurriedly Bond closes the safe, but Tibbett replaces the microchip in a different compartment. Zorin's warehouse reveals a hoard of microchips, even though there is a world surplus. Bond and Tibbett dispose of the guards in packing cases on a nearby conveyor belt. Zorin is working out with May Day when they are interrupted by Scarpine with the news of intruders in the warehouse. Bond narrowly manages to regain entry to the château as Zorin raises the drawbridge, but is unable to return to his room. Zorin and May Day enter Bond's bedroom to find it empty and she remembers he was the man at the Eiffel Tower.

Returning to her bedroom, May Day finds Bond in her bed. Slipping off her robe, she climbs in bed on top of him. Checking the lab, Scarpine and Dr Mortner discover someone has opened the safe.

In the morning, Bond is called into Zorin's office. Zorin is using his desktop computer to discover Bond's true identity. Zorin smiles as Bond's image appears on his computer and the words 'James Bond 007 Licensed to Kill' flash across the screen. Zorin asks Bond to accompany him on his morning ride. In the meantime, Bond asks Tibbett to contact M and put a trace on the cheque issued to Miss Sutton. Tibbett drives into town but, taking the Rolls through the car wash, he is killed by May Day.

ABOVE: *(left) Jumpin' jodhpurs! Jenny Flex (Alison Doody), not a girl to argue with, unless you're into bondage. (right) Pola (Fiona Fullerton) pops out of the night to pleasantly surprise 007 with a trip to the Nippon Relaxation Spa.*

Zorin's morning ride turns out to be a very rough experience. 007 finds himself covering a steeplechase course where the jumps are electronically raised and lengthened, and the exercise boys try to knock him from his horse. Zorin uses the remote-control transmitter on his whip to send Bond's horse wildly out of control. Chased through the woods by Scarpine and his men, Bond sees the Rolls. He jumps from his horse and hangs on to the car, only to find May Day is driving and Tibbett's body is slumped in the back seat. Bond is knocked unconscious and placed in the car with Tibbett, and May Day pushes the car into a nearby lake. The cold water rising around his body brings Bond back to consciousness and he escapes from the car. But Zorin and May Day are still standing at the lakeside, and Bond carefully breathes from the compressed air in the car tyres.

Zorin and May Day arrive in San Francisco by airship. Bond's contact there, CIA agent Chuck Lee, has identified the photographs taken by 007 at the château and reveals that Mortner's real identity is Hans Glaub, a German pioneer in the development of steroids. During World War II he had experimented with steroids on pregnant women in concentration camps to enhance intelligence. Virtually every mother aborted, although a handful of children were produced with phenomenal IQs. However, there was one side-effect – they were psychotic. Glaub was unable to be tried by the War Crimes Commission as the Russians grabbed him at the end of the war and set him up in a laboratory to develop steroids for their athletes. There is every chance that Zorin is the result of one of Glaub's experiments – and he is certainly psychotic.

That night Bond investigates Zorin's oil pumping station but, as he swims into the pipe, Zorin begins testing its efficiency, and Bond is almost drawn into the rotating blades of

the pump. Bond has noticed another diver, and swimming ashore discovers it to be Pola Ivanova. They drive to the Nippon Relaxation Spa, where they share a hot tub. 'That feels wonderful,' says Pola. 'Feels even better from where I'm sitting. Would you like it harder?' asked Bond, massaging her neck. Pola leaves with the tape she has recorded of Zorin's conversation in the control room while Bond is showering. But Bond has switched tapes and learns that something is going to happen in Silicon Valley in three days, but is puzzled by the name Mainstrike.

Posing as James Stock from the London *Financial Times*, Bond visits San Francisco City Hall to interview W. G. Howe, who is the head of the Department of Conservation for oil and mines. Bond discovers it is usual practice to pump sea water in to test the integrity of an oil pipeline. Stacey Sutton is also at City Hall and Bond follows her to a mansion on the outskirts of town, where he convinces her he is not a 'Zorin stooge' after driving off several of Zorin's thugs who break into her house. Stacey is a geologist who works for City Hall and is heir to Sutton Oil, which Zorin has taken from her in a rigged proxy fight. Knowing that her late father's oil company is worth far less than five million dollars, Stacey realizes Zorin has tried to buy her silence. 'I'd sell everything and live in a tent before I give up,' says Stacey, tearing up Zorin's cheque. She retires for the night, and Bond sleeps on guard in a chair. The next morning they experience a slight earth tremor and Bond mentions Zorin's water-pumping activities. Stacey explains that pumping sea water into a fault area is extremely dangerous, as flooding a fault could cause a major earthquake. She then tries to explain Zorin's plan to Howe – but he fires her.

Chuck Lee tells Bond that he must know Zorin's specific intentions before he can take it to his superiors but he is murdered by May Day as he leaves Stacey's house. That evening Bond and Stacey investigate the file room at City Hall. They discover that Mainstrike is an abandoned silver mine by the San Andreas fault. Suddenly Zorin bursts in with May Day, who disarms Bond. Howe is working late in his office. Zorin shoots him with Bond's gun and traps 007 and Stacey in an elevator. Zorin and May Day set the building on fire and abandon Bond and Stacey to their fate. Climbing through the service hatch of the elevator, Bond lifts Stacey to safety, but as they leave the burning building, Bond is arrested by a police captain who has found his gun at the scene of Howe's murder. Bond and Stacey escape in a fire truck and successfully elude the policemen when they drive over a rising drawbridge.

They drive to the Mainstrike mine, where the full extent of Zorin's plan is revealed. By flooding the faults Zorin can create a double earthquake, moving both fault lines at once, and submerging the whole of Silicon Valley for ever. With less than an hour before the culmination of Zorin's plan, Bond has to act fast, but May Day, Jenny Flex and Pan-Ho are after them. Zorin detonates the bombs set to flood the mine,

ABOVE: *Finding a workman's boiler suit 'just her size', Stacey and Bond discover Zorin's dastardly plan at the Mainstrike silver mine.*

sweeping Jenny Flex and Pan-Ho to their deaths. Zorin and Scarpine machine-gun the surviving miners. Stacey escapes up a shaft to the surface, but Bond is caught by May Day as they plunge into the raging flood waters. As the water subsides, Bond and May Day make for the cavern, where Zorin has planted a time bomb. If the bomb detonates, the huge amount of explosives beneath will rupture the geological lock which holds the faults together. Bond and May Day lift the bomb on to a railcar but, as they are trying to push it out of the mine, the handbrake jams. With Bond shouting at her to jump, May Day rides the railcar clear of the mine and the bomb explodes, killing her instantly.

In her excitement at seeing Bond alive, Stacey fails to notice Zorin is closing in on her in his airship. As he yanks her inside the dirigible, Bond clings to its mooring line for dear life. Zorin heads for the Golden Gate Bridge, where he intends to smash Bond against its girders. Bond lashes the mooring rope around the cables on the bridge while Stacey attacks Zorin. The airship gondola crashes into the bridge, knocking Mortner and Scarpine unconscious. Stacey leaps from the gondola on to the bridge as Zorin chases her with a fire axe. Bond and Zorin struggle violently on the bridge until Zorin loses his grip and falls to his death into the water far below. Having regained consciousness and witnessing the death of his prodigy, Mortner attempts to destroy Bond with a bundle of dynamite but Bond severs the mooring rope with the axe and the airship shudders violently as Mortner falls back into the gondola. An enormous explosion destroys the airship, taking Mortner and Scarpine with it.

Sharing a shower together, Bond and Stacey are interrupted by Q's robot snooper. Reporting to M, Q reports, '007 is alive – he's just cleaning up a few details!' Bond throws a towel over the snooper as he and Stacey disappear below the shower curtain. 'Oh, James,' sighs Stacey.

TANYA ROBERTS'S character, Stacey Sutton, is undoubtedly the most helpless of all the Bond Girls to date, as she hangs from Bond's arm squealing at every opportunity. While appearing in TV's *Vegas*, Tanya was seen by producer Aaron Spelling and was cast in *Charlie's Angels*. Her success in the show was immediate and she became a popular TV personality. She was the original choice to star opposite Dudley Moore in *'10'* but she was replaced at the last moment by Bo Derek. Her other movie appearances include *The Beastmaster* (1982) and *Sheena, Queen of the Jungle* (1984).

May Day was Grace Jones's second screen appearance after her debut in *Conan the Destroyer* (1984). This flamboyant and visually exciting singer/actress left her native Jamaica at the age of 18 for New York, where she worked as a model while auditioning for films and plays. She then moved to Paris and within three months was one of France's top models. Her first single, 'La Vie en Rose' went gold in France and Italy. She continued to cultivate her *avant-garde* image under the spell of French artist Jean Paul Goude. She made headline news when she hit chat-show host Russell Harty on his live TV show. Her other movie appearances include *Vamp* (1987).

Fiona Fullerton makes a brief but telling appearance as Pola Ivanova. She has one of the best lines in the film when she squeals, 'Oh, the bubbles tickle my – Tchaikovsky!' as Bond switches the cassette player on. Born in Nigeria, Fiona entered the film industry in 1968 at the age of 12 when she appeared in *Run Wild, Run Free*. Her other screen appearances include *Nicholas and Alexandra* (1971) and *Alice's Adventures in Wonderland* (1972). She has also appeared in the TV series *The Charmer, Angels* and *Dick Barton*. Her stage successes include *The Royal Baccarat Scandal*.

ABOVE: *(left) After offering to lead Stacey to the chopper, Bond is distracted by May Day.*
(right) The most beautiful iceberg driver in the world, Kimberley Jones
(Mary Stavin), aids 007's escape from Siberia.

ABOVE: *Stacey Sutton (Tanya Roberts), heir to Sutton Oil, geologist – and screamer!*

Britain's Last Line of Defence Miss Moneypenny

Lois Maxwell (1962-1985)

The only woman to regularly feature in the life of James Bond is, of course, Miss Moneypenny – portrayed in 14 of the Bond movies over 23 years by Canadian actress Lois Maxwell (born Lois Hooker in 1927). Her verbal sparring with Connery and Moore was a high point of the series and still amuses after countless viewings.

Starting her career in the same studio 'charm school' as Marilyn Monroe, Lois made her screen debut in *Spring Song* (1946). She has appeared in over 50 films and had many guest roles in TV series, including *The Saint, The Avengers* and *Randall and Hopkirk Deceased*. Her film appearances include *The Haunting* (1963), the James Bond spoof *Operation Kid Brother* (1967) – in which she co-starred with Sean Connery's brother Neil and other Bond actors Daniela Bianchi, Bernard Lee, Adolfo Celi and Anthony Dawson – *The Adventurers* (1970) and *Lost and Found* (1979). She wrote the 'Moneypenny' column in the *Toronto Sun* for many years and appeared in a TV commercial for Brook Street Bureau as M's famous secretary.

Always a great draw at the James Bond International Fan Club's events, Lois enjoys a popularity that has never waned over the years. Widowed in the 1960s, she has now effectively retired from acting and settled in Dorset to be near her daughter and grandchildren.

Caroline Bliss (1987-1989)

The Living Daylights (1987) introduced us to a new Miss Moneypenny in the delectable shape of National Theatre player Caroline Bliss. Her Moneypenny had more of a schoolgirl crush on the new Bond, Timothy Dalton, but was hardly likely to engage his romantic interest by offering him an evening listening to her Barry Manilow records.

Caroline originally studied dancing but later trained at the Bristol Old Vic Theatre School. Her first television role was as Princess Diana in *Charles and Diana, A Royal Love Story* for the USA's ABC TV. Her other TV appearances include *Chess Game, My Brother Jonathan* and *Dempsey and Makepeace*. She is the granddaughter of composer Sir Arthur Bliss, who was Master of the Queen's Music.

Samantha Bond (1995-   )

After a six-year break between James Bond films, 007 burst back on to cinema screens in 1995 with the record-breaking *GoldenEye*. And to accompany yet another Bond, this time in the svelte shape of Pierce Brosnan, was a new Moneypenny. Samantha Bond's Moneypenny is a consummate professional who complements her female boss, M, perfectly. As well as the distinct link between them in the chain of command, they also have a strong bond as women at the top of their profession in what is ostensibly a man's world.

Samantha is a member of the Royal Shakespeare Company and also played at the National Theatre in *The Cid*. Apart from the Bond movies, her only other film appearance was in *Erik the Viking* (1989). However, her career in TV has been prolific, with important roles in *The Bill, Poirot, Mr White Goes to Westminster, Emma* and the major BBC series *Tears Before Bedtime*. In 1999 she

ABOVE: *Lois Maxwell's Moneypenny receives a rare gift from 007 in* Octopussy *– a carnation.*

BELOW: *Their eyes adored her: Sean Connery turns on the charm in* Goldfinger*; the same old James, only more so. George Lazenby gets frisky in* On Her Majesty's Secret Service*; straight from the pampas, Roger Moore reports in to the South American office in* Moonraker*.*

appeared on Broadway with Dame Judi Dench in Sir David Hare's *Amy's View*, for which she was nominated for a Tony as Best Supporting Actress.

This lady's not for turning
Judi Dench – M (1995–   )

The most inspired casting choice in the history of the Bond series is without doubt Dame Judi Dench in the role of M. No other contemporary actress is able to leave such a lasting impression in such a short space of screen time, as witnessed by her 1999 Academy Award for Best Supporting Actress in *Shakespeare in Love*. Her initial portrayal of M in *GoldenEye* had us believe that her character felt only contempt for 007, her 'misogynist dinosaur' secret agent. But a final look of admiration and a 'come back alive' proved that, like all women, she had a soft spot for Bond.

Tomorrow Never Dies saw her more involved in the plot, and once again coming to the defence of her top agent for 'doing his job'. In *The World Is Not Enough*, M discovers for herself how much wear and tear goes on out there in the field, when roles are reversed and she is kidnapped by the very person she is trying to protect. Her strength and ability to execute her job are never more ably conveyed than when she discovers that MI6 have been manipulated into causing the death of her old friend Sir Robert King: 'This will not stand. We will not be terrorized by cowards who would murder an innocent man – and use us as the tool. We will find the people who committed this atrocity. We will hunt them, we will track them, we will follow them – to the far corners of the earth if need be – and we will bring them to justice.'

Simply put, Dame Judi Dench is a theatrical legend. She made her stage debut fresh from the Central School of Speech Training and Dramatic Art as Ophelia in the Old Vic's 1957 Liverpool production of *Hamlet*. It wasn't until 1961, when she joined the Royal Shakespeare Company, that her affinity with the Bard came to the fore, leading to her appearance in most of Shakespeare's major plays. In 1967 she played, to rave reviews, the hedonistic Sally Bowles in the London stage production of *Cabaret*, and also appeared in plays by George Bernard Shaw, Oscar Wilde and Chekhov, as well as in Stephen Sondheim's *A Little Night Music*, in which she delivered the memorable song 'Send in the Clowns'. In 1999 on Broadway she won a Tony award for Best Actress in the dramatic play *Amy's View*.

Her TV career has also been outstanding, with plays and series like *Going Gently*, *A Fine Romance* and *As Time Goes By* winning her three BAFTA awards for Best TV Actress.

Her first film award was a BAFTA for Most Promising Newcomer in 1965, in *Four in the Morning*, scored by John Barry. In recent years her film career has become more prolific, with starring roles in *A Room with a View* (BAFTA Award for Best Supporting Actress), *A Handful of Dust* (BAFTA Award for Best Supporting Actress), *Mrs Brown* (BAFTA Award for Best Actress, Scottish BAFTA Award for Best Actress, Golden Globe Award for Best Actress) and *Tea with Mussolini*.

ABOVE: *(top left) Caroline Bliss assists Timothy Dalton's 007 with a secret rendezvous in Bratislava in* The Living Daylights.
(top right) 'But you've never had me James!' Samantha Bond puts Pierce Brosnan's 007 severely in his place in GoldenEye.
INSET: *Judi Dench's role as M brought further insight to her character in* Tomorrow Never Dies.

The Living Daylights (1987)

JAMES BOND	TIMOTHY DALTON
KARA MILOVY	MARYAM d'ABO
GENERAL GEORGI KOSKOV	JEROEN KRABBE
BRAD WHITAKER	JOE DON BAKER
GENERAL LEONID PUSHKIN	JOHN RHYS-DAVIES
KAMRAN SHAH	ART MALIK
NECROS	ANDREAS WISNIEWSKI
SAUNDERS	THOMAS WHEATLEY
Q	DESMOND LLEWELYN
M	ROBERT BROWN
MISS MONEYPENNY	CAROLINE BLISS
PRODUCERS	ALBERT R. BROCCOLI
	MICHAEL G. WILSON
DIRECTOR	JOHN GLEN
SCREENPLAY	RICHARD MAIBAUM
	MICHAEL G. WILSON
PRODUCTION DESIGNED BY	PETER LAMONT
DIRECTOR OF PHOTOGRAPHY	ALEC MILLS

JAMES BOND unravels a complicated plot involving a KGB General, an international terrorist and an unscrupulous arms dealer.

After disposing of an assassin who has infiltrated a training mission on Gibraltar, James Bond travels to Bratislava, where he is assigned to protect the defecting General Koskov. That evening Bond attends a concert and is impressed by the attractive blonde cellist in the orchestra. His contact Saunders tells him everything is set for Koskov to make his run. Leaving the concert hall Bond and Saunders enter a closed building across the street and, once upstairs, Bond positions himself on the balcony with his sniper's rifle. He waits for the KGB sniper who will most certainly cut Koskov's run short if he does not get in the first shot. Through the telescopic sight of his rifle, Bond is surprised to see that the enemy sniper is the blonde cellist. Realizing that she is an amateur, Bond deliberately disobeys his orders to kill the sniper and instead shoots the gun from her hand. Koskov is literally shot across the border in a natural gas pipeline and flown by Harrier jet to England. Once home 007 asks Q and Moneypenny to see if they can discover any information about the female sniper.

ABOVE: *(left) Kara (Maryam d'Abo) is pleased to discover Bond (Timothy Dalton) in her dressing room after her first solo concert performance.*
(right) Even with a bullet hole in her cello, Kara makes sweet music.
OPPOSITE: *Kara cuts a romantic figure in the tribal costume of the Mujahedin.*

During his de-briefing with M at the Koskov safe house, Bond explains the note left on the body of the double-O agent murdered on Gibraltar means 'Death to Spies'. Koskov reveals that this is an assassination programme instigated by General Pushkin to remove all Western agents. Unbeknown to the gathering, Necros, an international terrorist, has infiltrated the house disguised as a milkman. As Bond and M leave for London, Necros strangles one guard and disposes of any further opposition with his explosive milk bottles, finally grabbing a reluctant Koskov and kidnapping him in a helicopter. After such a humiliation by the KGB, Bond is ordered to assassinate General Pushkin, but Bond knows

Pushkin to be a man of integrity and doubts he would instigate such an operation. Without M's knowledge Bond returns to Bratislava to investigate the blonde cellist. Waiting in her apartment, Bond discovers that her name is Kara and that she is Koskov's girlfriend. Kara believes Bond to be Koskov's friend and escapes with him in his gadget-laden Aston Martin.

In Tangier, arms dealer Brad Whitaker is visited at his villa by General Pushkin. Pushkin informs Whitaker that he knows Koskov and the arms dealer are planning something. He cancels his recent arms order and tells Whitaker to return the money in two days or he will put him out of business – permanently. Whitaker tells Koskov (who is kidnapped by Necros only to deceive the British) that his plan that Bond

should kill Pushkin does not seem to be working. Koskov suggests the death of another British agent will guarantee Pushkin's demise.

Bond and Kara are sightseeing in Vienna and they visit the funfair where 007 has arranged to meet Saunders. Leaving Kara on the pretext of receiving a message from Koskov, Bond keeps his appointment with Saunders in a nearby café – but Necros has booby-trapped the mechanism operating the café's sliding glass door. As Saunders leaves, Necros triggers an explosive device, sending the glass door scything into the unfortunate agent. Surveying the carnage, Bond sees a balloon bearing the words 'Smiert Spionam' – 'Death to Spies'. Bond returns to Kara, who asks if he has heard from Koskov. 'Yes, I

ABOVE: *(top) 007 is about to use Kara's Stradivarius cello, the Lady Rose, as part of a movement not taught at the conservatoire. (left) Kara is duped by the wily Koskov into drugging 007's vodka Martini. (right) All the fun of the fair! For a short while Bond and Kara share a romantic interlude.*

got the message,' says Bond, trying to control his anger. He tells Kara they must leave for Tangier immediately, where Koskov is waiting for her. Back in Tangier, Bond questions Pushkin at gunpoint about Koskov's allegations. Satisfied that Pushkin is an innocent party, Bond is now sure of his true quarry. Bond accepts Pushkin's suggestion that Bond should fake his assassination. Believing the Soviet general is dead, Koskov tricks Kara into drugging Bond, and Koskov and Necros board a Russian transport plane, taking Kara and the drugged Bond with them. Bond and Kara are transferred to the jail of a Russian air base in Afghanistan but Bond disables the guards with Kara's help and they escape over the perimeter fence with a fellow prisoner.

Bond and Kara are captured by a local group of Mujahedin tribesmen and discover their fellow prisoner is Kamran Shah, the group's leader. Unable to enlist Kamran's help, Bond is forced to accompany the tribesmen on a drug deal in the desert. At the rendezvous he discovers the buyer is Koskov, who is financing the deal with the down payment of the arms money. Hiding in the drug-laden trucks, Bond is driven back to the air base and assists in loading the cargo into the transport plane – where he plants a bomb. However, Koskov and Necros recognize him and Bond is trapped inside the aircraft. Kamran and his men attack the air base as Bond

hijacks the transport plane. During the ensuing battle, Kara drives into the hold of the aircraft, pursued by Necros and Koskov, and joins Bond in the cockpit as the plane takes off – unaware that Necros is aboard. Kara takes the controls while Bond returns to the hold to defuse his bomb, but he is suddenly attacked from behind by Necros. Panicking at the controls, Kara accidentally opens the loading ramp, and the netted cargo of drugs trails from the plane with the two men hanging on. After a desperate struggle Necros is left clinging on to Bond's boot. Drawing a knife, Bond cuts his bootlaces and the unfortunate killer plunges to his death. Bond then defuses the bomb, resets the timer and drops it on the Russian troops pursuing Kamran and his men. Returning to the flight deck,

ABOVE: *(top) General Pushkin's lady friend, Rubavitch (Virginia Hey), is unaware of the assassins waiting in the wings. (bottom) Kara is thrilled to be out on the town with Bond.*

Bond discovers the aircraft is running out of fuel. He sends Kara into the Jeep secured in the hold, lowers the ramp and fires the release mechanism. As the aircraft is about to crash, the Jeep is jettisoned from the rear of the plane and Bond and Kara safely crash-land.

Whitaker is in his villa in Tangier, where Bond finds him playing with his model soldiers. Bond is knocked to the floor and Whitaker attacks him with an armoured machine-gun. Placing his explosive keyfinder on a bust of Wellington, Bond dodges Whitaker's bullets as Q's handy gadget detonates. The bust crashes down on the arms dealer, killing him instantly. 'He met his Waterloo,' Bond says drily to Pushkin as he enters the room. Koskov is apparently overjoyed at seeing Pushkin, but his good humour is short-lived when the Soviet General orders him sent home – in the diplomatic bag!

After a hugely successful concert, Kara returns to her dressing room and is overjoyed to find that Bond has not missed her performance after all.

KARA MILOVY is unusual for a Bond Girl in that she is a more vulnerable and naïve character than the kind of women that 007 usually associates with, and this is probably the reason why James Bond warms to her character. Born in London of a Dutch father and a Russian (Georgian) mother, Maryam d'Abo left England at the age of five and was brought up and educated in Paris and Geneva. French is her mother tongue, although she speaks English fluently without a trace of an accent. She claims it was her reaction to the Bond movies at the age of 11 that made her want to be an actress. Maryam returned to London in 1980 to study at the Drama Centre, and has since appeared in such films as *White Nights*, *Lime Street* and *Until September*. She has also appeared on TV in commercials and the mini-series *Master of the Game*.

ABOVE: *(left) Timothy Dalton and Maryam d'Abo share a joke with the crew during filming.*
(right) Breathless! Rosika Miklos (Julie T. Wallace) creates a 'diversion' so that
007 can successfully carry out his mission.

ABOVE: *(top) Linda (Kell Tyler) is bored until 007 drops in by parachute.*
(left) After hitting Pushkin, 007 uses Rubavitch to distract the General's guard.
(right) Although popular opinion considered Timothy Dalton's
Bond a 'new man', 007 still had women falling at his feet.

Licence To Kill (1989)

JAMES BOND	TIMOTHY DALTON
PAM BOUVIER	CAREY LOWELL
FRANZ SANCHEZ	ROBERT DAVI
LUPE LAMORA	TALISA SOTO
MILTON KREST	ANTHONY ZERBE
JOE BUTCHER	WAYNE NEWTON
Q	DESMOND LLEWELYN
FELIX LEITER	DAVID HEDISON
DELLA CHURCHILL	PRISCILLA BARNES
M	ROBERT BROWN
MISS MONEYPENNY	CAROLINE BLISS
HELLER	DON STROUD
PRODUCERS	ALBERT R. BROCCOLI
	MICHAEL G. WILSON
DIRECTOR	JOHN GLEN
SCREENPLAY	MICHAEL G. WILSON
	RICHARD MAIBAUM
PRODUCTION DESIGNED BY	PETER LAMONT
DIRECTOR OF PHOTOGRAPHY	ALEC MILLS

JAMES BOND sets out on a personal vendetta against a billionaire drug lord in South America. Bond is on leave in the Florida Keys, where he is about to be the best man at the wedding of his old CIA friend Felix Leiter to Della Churchill. On their way to the church in Key West, Bond, Leiter and his fisherman buddy, Sharkey, are stopped by a Coast Guard helicopter swooping down to report that billionaire drug lord Franz Sanchez is at this moment within reach in the nearby Bahamas. Leiter, who has left the CIA and is now in charge of the Drug Enforcement Agency office in the south of Florida, has been desperate to get his hands on Sanchez – a vicious criminal, invulnerable under the protection of bought politicians in a small banana republic in Latin America. Now armed with extradition papers, Leiter has a real chance to capture his nemesis. The wedding must wait. Leiter, with Bond's help, captures Sanchez after an exciting land and air chase that ends with Bond literally reeling in Sanchez's single-engined aircraft while dangling beneath the Coast Guard helicopter. Bond and Leiter eventually arrive at the church by parachute.

No sooner is Sanchez in custody than a cleverly organized escape is engineered by a group whose leader is Milton Krest, who operates out of Key West behind the cover of a marine biology laboratory and the research vessel the *Wavekrest*. Sanchez returns to safety in his Latin American headquarters in Isthmus City, but not before exacting a horrible revenge on Leiter and Della. As Bond is about to fly back to London to return to duty, he learns of Sanchez's escape and immediately drives to Leiter's home, where he discovers Della dead and Felix mutilated and barely alive. Certain that not enough will be done by the Drug Enforcement Agency, because of the extradition problems, Bond decides to go after Sanchez on his own – he will make it his personal mission to bring down the vicious drug lord and is willing to sacrifice his own career as a double-O agent if necessary.

When M arrives in Key West to remind Bond that the capture of Sanchez is an American matter and he must forget about it, Bond refuses and is told that his licence to kill is summarily revoked and he must hand in his PPK. Bond refuses, eludes his fellow agents and sets off on his own. Learning from Sharkey that Leiter's wounds were most probably caused by a man-eating shark, Bond, with the help of the burly fisherman, follows a trail that eventually leads to Krest's marine biology lab. He not only discovers it is where Leiter was tortured but finds the renegade US Marshall Killifer, who, thanks to a two-million-dollar bribe, was a key player in arranging Sanchez's clever escape. Bond makes certain that Killifer is killed by the same shark that attacked Leiter.

Bond's next move is to slip aboard the *Wavekrest* in the hope that it will lead him further into the heart of the Sanchez drug empire. He encounters the seductive and beautiful Lupe, Sanchez's sometime girlfriend. Though always in fear of

ABOVE: *Attending the wedding of his friends Felix Leiter (David Hedison) and Della Churchill (Priscilla Barnes) as Best Man, Bond (Timothy Dalton) is touched by their gift of a cigarette lighter.*

Sanchez and his fits of murderous temper, she agrees to help the handsome stranger.

In Isthmus City Sanchez owns not only the casino, but the banks and practically everything else, including the corrupt government run by President Hector Lopez. Bond enlists the aid of one of Leiter's key contacts, the exquisite Pam Bouvier, a freelance charter pilot who has flown for both the US Army and the CIA front Air America. Bearing suitcases stuffed with millions of dollars of drug money 'recovered' from the *Wavekrest*, Bond and Pam fly to Isthmus City, where they set up residence in style in a luxurious suite in the top hotel. He quickly discovers that Sanchez's bank and gambling casino are fronts for a sophisticated money-laundering operation. Among Sanchez's principal accomplices are his financial adviser, Truman-Lodge, knife-throwing thug Dario and a former American Green Beret, Colonel Heller. As a means of broadcasting drug-dealing prices to his international network, Sanchez works through a flamboyant television fund-raiser named Joe Butcher, leader of a cult espousing the secrets of 'cone-power', headquartered at the nearby Olimpatec Meditation Institute. As part of his plan to enlarge his evil empire to every corner of the globe, Sanchez arranges for a group of Oriental businessmen headed by Kwang to arrive for discussions about collaborating with his organization in order to bring the drug trade in the whole of Asia under his control.

At the gambling casino with his 'secretary' Pam, Bond uses the pliable Lupe to arrange a meeting with Sanchez. 007 readily discloses his true identity and his present situation, a former British agent seeking employment with a generous patron. Sanchez is intrigued but advises Bond that he has all

ABOVE: *(left) Beautiful in blue! Carey Lowell was without doubt one of the most sensual of all the Bond Girls.*
(right) Lupe (Talisa Soto) has definite plans for 007.

the help he needs. While Bond plots how to break through Sanchez's formidable defences, reinforcements arrive from London. Moneypenny has told Q the reasons for Bond's dismissal from the Service, so Q decides, without authorization, to take his holiday leave and shows up in Isthmus City with a bag of lethal tricks. Bond sets upon a plan to kill Sanchez and is about to pull the trigger when he is unexpectedly captured by Kwang and his accomplice, Loti. They are undercover narcotics agents from Hong Kong and have spent years to reach the point where they have finally been able to penetrate the Sanchez organization. Bond's 'rogue-agent' theatrics have threatened to blow their plan of penetrating the heart of Sanchez's drug kingdom. Bond killing him would not stop his trade in death! Suddenly Heller and a detachment of the Isthmus City army arrive at the safe-house and Kwang and his people are annihilated.

Heller and Sanchez find 007 among the rubble and Sanchez, now convinced of Bond's sincerity, takes him to his palatial home to recover. Knowing that the *Wavekrest* is about to dock in Isthmus City, Bond is able to persuade Sanchez that Milton Krest has been double-crossing him. Bond cleverly does a 'sting' on Krest, and as a result Sanchez sends Krest to a horrible death. Reluctantly, Bond accepts Q's desire to be a field operative for the first time, and together with Pam and Lupe, each in their own way helping him, they slowly begin to chip away at the very foundations of Sanchez's organization. Sanchez decides to clinch his deal with the Orientals by showing them the heart of Joe Butcher's Olimpatec Meditation Institute. Still considering Bond a loyal lieutenant, he brings him along to assist in a major operation he has planned. Beneath the institute is a secret laboratory where Sanchez has ingeniously had research chemists successfully working on a formula that would allow cocaine to be dissolved in gasoline and then later be converted back to powder. Until it reached its destination, it would appear to be no more than an innocent

ABOVE: *(left) With only a pet iguana to remind her of Sanchez, Lupe (Talisa Soto)*
is after a husband, in the shape of James Bond.

ABOVE & INSET: *Costume designer Jodie Tillen used Carey Lowell's fabulous figure to full advantage in the outfits she wore in* Licence To Kill.

shipment of petrol. A fleet of tanker trucks are being prepared to transport the shipment to the coast to be loaded on ships heading for the Orient.

Bond finally shows his hand and Sanchez realizes that his 'friend' is in fact his deadly enemy as the convoy heads for port with its lethal cargo. With the help of Pam, flying a tiny crop-duster aeroplane, Bond eventually faces Sanchez in a bloody duel to the death, but not before Bond makes certain that Sanchez knows that it has all been personal.

BORN ON 11 February 1961 in New York, Carey Lowell was one of America's leading fashion models working with top designers Calvin Klein and Ralph Lauren. She began modelling part-time while attending the University of Colorado, and it was during this time that her 5 ft 10 in caught the attention of a representative of the prestigious Ford Model Agency in New York. She lived in France for a brief period before deciding to continue her college education and modelling career. She won the part of Pam Bouvier after an extensive search for the first Bond Girl embodying the spirit of the 1990s. Her acting debut was in *Club Paradise* (1986) with Robin Williams and soon after she appeared in *Dangerously Close* (1986), *Downtwisted* (1987) and *Me and Him* (1988). She also appeared as a regular for three years in *Law and Order* on US TV.

Licence To Kill was only the second screen appearance for leading American fashion model Talisa Soto. Her first was in *Spike of Bensonhurst*, directed by cult director Paul Morrissey. At the age of 15, with no previous experience, Talisa became a fashion model with one of New York's top agencies. She literally walked in off the street, looking for a summer job. Within a week, she was in Paris being photographed by Bruce Weber for *Vogue* magazine. Born Miriam Soto in Brooklyn on 27 March 1967, she has decided to cut down on her modelling work while concentrating on her film career. More recently she appeared as a regular in the US TV series *Hearts of the West*, and in the cinema release *Mortal Kombat*.

ABOVE: *(left) Talisa Soto and Carey Lowell pose with villain Robert Davi for a provocative publicity shot.*
(right) Licence To Kill was filmed at Churubusco Studios in Mexico City, where this shot of Carey Lowell was taken.

ABOVE: (top left) Diana Lee-Hsu appeared as Loti, a beautiful but deadly Hong Kong undercover narcotics agent. (top right) Loti and her partner Kwang (Cary-Hiroyuki Tagawa) discover that Bond has inadvertently wrecked their plan to arrest Sanchez.
BOTTOM: (left) Lupe is as much a prisoner of Sanchez (Robert Davi), as she is his girlfriend. (right) Ravishing in red! Talisa Soto's modelling credentials are ably demonstrated in this publicity shot.

The Bad and the Beautiful . . .

. . . and the Less Beautiful

ABOVE: *(left) Rosa Klebb (Lotte Lenya) has designs on Tania's curvaceous form in* From Russia With Love.
(right) Irma Bunt (Ilse Steppat) welcomes a disguised 007 to Blofeld's mountaintop lair On Her Majesty's Secret Service.

ABOVE: *(top left) Naomi (Caroline Munro) tried a fly-by shooting to riddle OO7 with bullet's from her helicopter in* The Spy Who Loved Me *(1977).*
(top right) The terrible trio of Jenny Flex (Alison Doody), May Day (Grace Jones), and Pan Ho (Papillon Soo Soo) meant triple trouble for OO7 in
A View To A Kill *(1985). (bottom) Xenia Onatopp (Famke Janssen) enjoyed a good squeeze in* GoldenEye *(1995).*
OPPOSITE: *(top left) Mai Ling (Mai Ling) attempts to spy on Bond during his flight on Goldfinger's jet, but OO7 foils her with a handy can of shaving foam.*
(top right) Road rage with a vengeance! Fiona Volpe (Luciana Paluzzi) certainly burned up anyone who got in her way.

JAMES BOND battles with renegade Russian forces who threaten to destroy the world's social and financial fabric with the aid of an outer space weapons system, code-named Goldeneye.

Bond and 006, his friend and colleague Alec Trevelyan, join forces to penetrate a secret, mountain-top Soviet Nerve Gas Facility. They are detected and Trevelyan is captured by Commander Ourumov. Bond escapes, grabbing a military motorcycle and taking off in a hail of Russian bullets to pursue a light plane heading towards take-off from the landing strip hundreds of feet above the valley floor. As the limpet mines Bond planted earlier explode, destroying the chemical factory, the aircraft surges over the edge of the precipice and James Bond accelerates after it, over the cliff edge.

Nine years later, Bond is behind the wheel of his Aston Martin DB5, speeding along the mountain roads above Monte

GoldenEye (1995)

JAMES BOND	PIERCE BROSNAN
ALEXANDER TREVELYAN	SEAN BEAN
NATALYA SIMONOVA	IZABELLA SCORUPCO
XENIA ONATOPP	FAMKE JANSSEN
JACK WADE	JOE DON BAKER
VALENTIN ZUKOVSKY	ROBBIE COLTRANE
MISHKIN	TCHEKY KARYO
OURUMOV	GOTTFRIED JOHN
BORIS GRISHENKO	ALAN CUMMING
TANNER	MICHAEL KITCHEN
CAROLINE	SERENA GORDON
Q	DESMOND LLEWELYN
MISS MONEYPENNY	SAMANTHA BOND
IRINA	MINNIE DRIVER
and	
M	JUDI DENCH
PRODUCERS	MICHAEL G. WILSON
	BARBARA BROCCOLI
DIRECTOR	MARTIN CAMPBELL
STORY	MICHAEL FRANCE
SCREENPLAY	JEFFREY CAINE AND BRUCE FEIRSTEIN
PRODUCTION DESIGNED BY	PETER LAMONT
DIRECTOR OF PHOTOGRAPHY	PHIL MEHEUX

Carlo. His attractive passenger is Caroline, sent from London by the new M to complete an evaluation on 007. In his rear-view mirror Bond notices a red Ferrari racing towards him, driven by a ravishingly beautiful woman. Driving parallel, Bond and the mystery woman exchange smiles and begin a duel of driving skills. Finally, Bond is outmanoeuvred by his unknown opponent and she accelerates away into the distance.

That evening, Bond arrives at the casino in Monte Carlo to find the red Ferrari parked outside and its mystery driver within. Bond buys her a drink, introduces himself at the baccarat table and discovers with some amusement that she is Georgian-Russian and called Xenia Onatopp. Everyone has declined to bet against Xenia until Bond calls 'Banco.' 'It appears we share the same passions. Three, anyway,' suggests Bond. 'I count two,' replies Xenia, 'motoring and baccarat. I

ABOVE: *(left) Caroline (Serena Gordon) experiences a hair-raising ride with 007 (Pierce Brosnan) in his Aston Martin DB5. (right) Natalya (Izabella Scorupco) escapes from the destruction at Severnaya.*

ABOVE: *You know the name. You know the number. A whole new lease of life was breathed into the 007 character when Pierce Brosnan took over the role. And with actresses of the calibre of Izabella Scorupco and Famke Janssen backing him up, Pierce didn't put a foot wrong.*

hope your third is where your real talent lies.' Before they can continue their conversation, Xenia leaves with Canadian Admiral Chuck Farrell.

Bond receives a message from Moneypenny via the on-board computer system in his DB5, and discovers Xenia is an ex-Soviet fighter-pilot with suspected links to the Janus Crime Syndicate located in St Petersburg. Later that night, on the luxury yacht *Manticore*, Xenia kills Farrell in her own special way – as they make love, she crushes his spine between her thighs. With an accomplice posing as Farrell, she then kills the crew of the Tiger, a state-of-the-art stealth helicopter which is NATO's latest deterrent, and pilots their aircraft out from under the noses of the French Navy.

The helicopter lands outside the Severnaya Station, a secret underground installation in Siberia which houses the Soviet space weapons research centre. Inside the centre, Xenia massacres the staff with her machine-gun. Only two escape.

Computer whiz-kid Boris Grishenko had been smoking a cigarette outside; he disappears. Natalya Fyodorovna Simonova, a computer programmer, had been in the kitchen; at the sound of the gunfire she hides in a storage cabinet.

Ourumov unlocks the arming device of the Goldeneye rogue satellite, Petya, and programmes it to fire at the station in a matter of minutes. He and Xenia take off again in the helicopter. In space, the satellite sheds its camouflage, revealing it to be an electromagnetic-pulse strike weapon. A huge magnetic pulse from the explosion destroys the satellite dish on the control centre and also three MiGs, scrambled to investigate the blast. Natalya escapes through the roof of the centre into the freezing Arctic weather.

Back in England, Bond is briefed by the new, female, M. She tells him that both British and American satellites were

knocked out in the nuclear blast, and that the Goldeneye is an electromagnetic-pulse strike satellite which creates a radiation surge that destroys anything with an electronic circuit within a 50-mile radius. Moscow have explained away the incident as an accident during a routine training exercise. M believes the Janus Syndicate are involved, and the only traceable link to them is Xenia Onatopp, although Bond's old enemy Ourumov is believed to have been responsible for the breakdown in security at Severnaya. James Bond is briefed to penetrate the local arms Mafia in Russia, seek out Janus, reassure the current Kremlin leadership and somehow being Ourumov to justice. However, M warns Bond there must be no personal vendetta – avenging Alec Trevelyan will not bring him back.

After a visit to see Q for some new death-defying gadgets, 007 flies to St Petersburg. With the help of CIA

ABOVE: *Much deadlier than the male! Xenia Onatopp (Famke Janssen) enjoys her work,*
whether it's shooting a couple of unsuspecting pilots,
or trying to squeeze the living daylights out of 007.

contact Jack Wade, he searches out erstwhile KGB controller turned weapons mogul Valentin Zukovsky, and introduces himself by pressing cold steel to Zukovsky's temple. 'Walther PPK 7.6mm. Lethal at 100 paces,' says Zukovsky. 'Only three men I know use that gun . . . and I believe I've killed two of them.'

Meanwhile, Natalya has made it to St Petersburg and, tracing Boris through his computer e-mail, manages to arrange an assignation with her erstwhile colleague. Before she can question him about his escape from Severnaya she is seized from behind by Xenia.

At the Grand St Petersburg Hotel, Bond senses the presence of an intruder in the steam room – Xenia. Following a brief but passionate struggle, he escapes her deathly grip and, holding a gun to her head, he demands to be taken to Janus.

Xenia drives Bond to an industrial park full of statues of former Soviet leaders, where a figure walks out from behind

Suddenly a dart is fired into Bond's neck and he falls to the ground, unconscious. He comes round to find himself tied into a seat inside the Tiger helicopter, with Natalya shouting at him from the seat behind. Realizing they are in the line of an incoming missile attack, he head-butts the control console and they are ejected to safety. They are picked up by Russian troops and questioned by Mishkin, the Russian Defence Minister. Natalya tells him that Ourumov was the traitor at Severnaya and that the explosion was set off by him – at which point Ourumov bursts in, grabs Bond's gun from the table and shoots Mishkin and his bodyguard dead.

Bond grabs the dead guard's Kalashnikov and blasts his way out of the building. Natalya is recaptured and bundled into a car driven by Ourumov. 007 commandeers a 36-ton Russian T55 tank and pursues them around St Petersburg, demolishing cars, statues and buildings in the chase. Ourumov manages to drag Natalya aboard Janus's mobile headquarters in

one of the massive tributes which are stored there. One side of the man's face is scarred. He greets Bond with a sneer, calling him 'Her Majesty's loyal terrier'. It is Alec Trevelyan. Stunned, Bond begins to understand that Trevelyan is Janus, a descendant of the Lienz Cossacks, a group which had fought for the Nazis against Russia in World War II. At the end of the war they surrendered to the British, expecting to join their war against Communism. Instead they were sent back to Stalin, who executed them. Trevelyan explains that his parents had escaped the execution squads but committed suicide in shame. The British government had made the mistake of thinking Trevelyan must have been too young to remember. In Trevelyan's twisted imagination, Bond's failure to save him on their mission parallels the British government's treachery to his parents.

a hyper-sophisticated armoured train, where they join Xenia and Trevelyan.

As the train moves off, Bond manoeuvres the tank into a railway tunnel, emerging to fire point blank at the oncoming engine; and as the train crashes into the tank, Bond enters the rear carriage and holds up Xenia and Trevelyan, who have been temporarily stunned by the impact of the crash. Ourumov enters with Natalya, holding a gun to her head. Bond shoots Ourumov dead but Xenia and Trevelyan escape. Armoured sheathing slams down over the windows. Bond has just three minutes to find a way out before the whole communication car detonates. He uses the laser beam in his watch to cut a hole in the armour-plated floor. Natalya manages to track the Janus command centre on its own computer network, just before she and Bond drop to freedom.

ABOVE: (left) 'Boys with toys'. Bond and Natalya fight their way out of a Russian military base.
(right) Natalya asks Bond how he can be so cold. 'It's what keeps me alive,' he replies.
'No. It's what keeps you alone', she counters.

110

Acting on information from Trevelyan's computer, Bond and Natalya head for Cuba. On reconnaissance above the jungle, their light aircraft is disabled by a surface-to-air missile. 007 comes to a clearing at the edge of a lake, face to face with Xenia, who is harnessed and suspended from an attack helicopter. Bond opens fire, panicking the pilot, who swerves away, thereby slamming Xenia into the fork of a tree, where she is crushed to death.

Suddenly, a huge latticed structure rises from the centre of the lake, and the water recedes as a parabolic dish, 1,000 feet in diameter, emerges from the lake bed. Bond and Natalya vault on to the dish and find themselves sliding helter-skelter towards the centre, dodging bullets shot by the guards who surround them. They hurtle out of control into the sump hole at the centre of the dish, which has easy access to the control centre itself. There they discover the true mission of Janus: to break into world banks by computer and transfer money electronically seconds before the one remaining Goldeneye satellite, Mischa, is set off to erase any record of the transactions. All the computer systems of the world's financial centres will go down, reducing global financial markets to nothing but blank screens.

In the ensuing battle, Boris discovers the Caribbean can be as cold as hell, and 007 finds he needs a head for heights for his final confrontation with Alec Trevelyan – a challenge which for 007 has become not only a matter of 'for Queen and country' but also a very personal affair.

NATALYA SIMONOVA in *GoldenEye* was Izabella Scorupco's first English-speaking role. Born in 1970 in the Polish village of Bialystok, close to the Russian border, she lived there with her mother, a doctor. In 1978, they moved to a

ABOVE: *(top) Hot work! Xenia enjoys a rough and tumble more than most girls – much to the chagrin of 007.*
(bottom) Irina (Minnie Driver), Zukovsky's mistress and tone-deaf nightclub 'singer'.

suburb outside Stockholm. Aged 17, Izabella became a teenage idol after appearing in a movie called *No One Can Love Like Us*. She developed her singing talent and her 1989 single, 'Substitute' and subsequent album *Iza* both reached gold in Sweden. In 1994, Izabella resumed acting and won the lead role in *Petri Tears* (1995).

Famke Janssen, who plays the deadly Xenia Onatopp, was born in Holland, began her professional career as a model, working at one time for Yves Saint Laurent. She now lives in California. After attending Columbia University and studying stagecraft with Harold Gushkin, she moved to Los Angeles and appeared in television series such as *Melrose Place*. Her first starring role in a major motion picture was in *Lords of Illusion* (1995) and since *GoldenEye* her films have included *The Faculty*, *Deep Rising* and *Celebrity*.

Serena Gordon – who plays Caroline, sent to Monte Carlo by M to evaluate Bond – trained at the Royal Academy of Dramatic Art in London, after which she joined the Regent's Park Open Air Theatre Company, with whom she toured the Middle East. Her first role was in the Merchant – Ivory film *Maurice*, and she has appeared regularly on stage and on British television.

Minnie Driver, appearing as nightclub chanteuse Irina, attended the Webber Douglas Theatre School in London. She has made frequent appearances on British television, while her feature film career really took off after *GoldenEye* with starring roles in *Circle of Friends*, *Grosse Point Blank*, *Good Will Hunting* and *An Ideal Husband*.

ABOVE: *(left) Dressed to kill! Famke Janssen, the sophisticated femme fatale of the 1990s.*
(right) Although the character of Natalya was a low-paid Russian computer programmer, she was at least allowed one exotic outfit by costume designer Lindy Hemming.

Tomorrow Never Dies (1997)

JAMES BOND	PIERCE BROSNAN
ELLIOT CARVER	JONATHAN PRYCE
WAI LIN	MICHELLE YEOH
PARIS CARVER	TERI HATCHER
GUPTA	RICKY JAY
STAMPER	GOTZ OTTO
Q	DESMOND LLEWELYN
MISS MONEYPENNY	SAMANTHA BOND
ROBINSON	COLIN SALMON
ADMIRAL ROEBUCK	GEOFFREY PALMER
GENERAL BUKHARIN	TERENCE RIGBY
MINISTER OF DEFENCE	JULIAN FELLOWES
TAMARA KELLY	NINA YOUNG
PROFESSOR BERGSTROM	CECILIE THOMSEN
DR KAUFMAN	VINCENT SCHIAVELLI
ADMIRAL KELLY	MICHAEL BYRNE
AVIS AGENT	ANJTE SCHMIDT
and	
M	JUDI DENCH
PRODUCERS	MICHAEL G. WILSON
	BARBARA BROCCOLI
DIRECTOR	ROGER SPOTTISWOODE
STORY	BRUCE FEIRSTEIN
SCREENPLAY	BRUCE FEIRSTEIN
PRODUCTION DESIGNER	ALLAN CAMERON
DIRECTOR OF PHOTOGRAPHY	ROBERT ELSWIT

JAMES BOND battles media mogul Elliot Carver in his apparent bid to start World War III.

After the British naval vessel HMS *Devonshire* has apparently been sunk by Chinese planes, M sends for agent 007. Studying a new language at Oxford University with linguist Professor Inga Bergstrom, 007 is telephoned by Miss Moneypenny. He is needed at the headquarters of the Ministry of Defence immediately. Agent 007's mission is to discover if a signal sent from one of Carver's communication satellites was involved with the sinking of the ship. Much to his displeasure, 007 is ordered to use his past relationship with Carver's wife, Paris, if it will aid the investigation. M tells 007 he has only 48 hours in which to prove the connection before Britain will take decisive action against the Chinese.

Arriving at Hamburg airport, Bond collects his hire car, a BMW 750i, from Q. He briefs Bond on its many gadgets, including a new cell phone which can operate the car by remote control, among other things. At Carver's party in his media headquarters, during which he will broadcast a declaration of his humanitarian principles, Bond, posing as a banker, meets the media mogul. The two men take an instant dislike to each other. Bond also meets an attractive Oriental woman, Wai Lin, who says she's a reporter. During the party Bond manages to meet Paris in a quiet corner, where it is apparent to both of them that the embers of their relationship have far from cooled. As they return to the party they are greeted by Carver, who has noticed their discreet rendezvous. Bond realizes that Paris is both frightened of and desperate to please Carver. While Carver starts his TV broadcast Bond is given a tour of the building and is escorted into a recording studio where Carver's security guards attack him. 007 deals with the guards and pulls the circuit breakers on the CMGN newsroom, where the media mogul is cut off in mid-sentence as the newsroom is plunged into darkness.

ABOVE: *(top) As their mission draws them closer together Wai Lin (Michelle Yeoh) finds herself more and more attracted to the Western agent 007 (Pierce Brosnan).*
(right) Professor Bergstrom (Cecilie Thomsen) enlarges 007's vocabulary.

Back in his hotel bedroom, Bond, gun in hand, waits apprehensively for the assailant that Carver will inevitably send. He is pleasantly surprised when Paris appears in the doorway. She has come to warn him that her husband is on to him. Their eyes lock and a passionate embrace follows. Later, Bond and Paris dress as she tells him about a secret laboratory on the top floor of the CMGN complex. Unknown to Bond and Paris, Carver's techno-terrorist associate, Henry Gupta, has played back their conversation from the security video to Carver. Checking Bond's employment record, Gupta believes it to be *too* perfect, pointing to his being a government agent.

While investigating the secret laboratory Bond is unaware that Carver and Stamper, the vicious head of CMGN security, have ordered the murder of Paris. Bond escapes from the laboratory after finding Wai Lin also breaking into the complex. She leaves in spectacular style as 007 takes on a number of Stamper's security guards. Bond has taken a GPS encoder from the lab safe, equipment which could have been involved in sending a misleading signal to HMS *Devonshire*. Returning to his hotel room, he is overwhelmed with grief and

ABOVE: *(top left) Handcuffed to each other, Bond and Wai Lin enjoy a refreshing shower in a Vietnamese back street.*
(top right) Michelle Yeoh portrays Colonel Wai Lin with a nod to the modern woman.
(bottom left) Oxford professors have never looked like this! Cecilie Thomsen as Professor Inga Bergstrom.
(bottom right) 007 and Wai Lin ride for their lives over the rooftops of Saigon.

anger at finding Paris strangled in his bed. A soft voice from the bathroom snaps 007 out of his immediate grief. It is Dr Kaufman, a hired killer who specializes in making murder look like suicide. Carver has planned to make Bond the suicide victim in his murder/suicide plot to shift blame for his wife's murder. When Stamper phones Kaufman to get Bond to open his heavily protected BMW in the hotel car park, 007 tricks the murderous doctor into using Q's ingenious cell phone so that the stun gun inside goes off in his hands. Giving Bond the edge he needed, he shoots Kaufman dead with his own gun. Bond escapes after an amazing car chase in the hotel multi-storey car park involving 007's BMW.

Landing at a US air force base in Okinawa, Commander James Bond, RN, has brought the GPS encoder with him to seek advice from the air force's expert, Dr Greenwalt. The scientist explains to Bond that, in theory, if someone altered the timing chip in the decoder it could slowly send a ship off course – similar to putting a magnet next to a compass. Checking on the *Devonshire's* last position, they calculate exactly where she sank. 007 parachutes into the sea in search of the sunken Royal Naval vessel.

Bond discovers HMS *Devonshire* 200 feet below on the ocean floor, with a large hole literally drilled in her hull, and Wai Lin investigating the wreck. They barely escape with their lives as the ship slides into a deep sea trench. Returning to the surface they are captured by Stamper and his men. Handcuffed together, Bond and Wai Lin are flown to Carver's Saigon headquarters. Outside Carver's office they

are passed in the corridor by Chinese soldiers in civilian clothes, and a Chinese man with an air of military command. Wai Lin registers alarm. She covers it – but not before Bond has seen her reaction. They are brought before Carver, who is sitting at a computer screen writing their obituaries: 'British Secret Service Agent James Bond and his collaborator Wai Lin of the Chinese People's External Security Force were found dead today in Vietnam.' Bond realizes Carver is quite insane. The media mogul hopes to achieve global domination by influencing the minds of people over the entire world through his media empire, which, after the final part of his plan is put into effect, will have more people under his influence than anyone else has achieved in the history of the planet. Carver leaves Bond and Wai Lin in the sadistic hands of Stamper, who prepares to torture them to death. Before Stamper can use a selection of grotesque surgical instruments on the couple, they shatter a window and leap for their lives. Landing on a deck one storey below, Bond and Wai Lin, holding the ropes from a banner, take an unbelievable leap over the edge of the building, ripping the banner, which slows their descent as they fall. Still handcuffed together, Bond and Wai Lin elude Stamper's security men on a motorcycle, while they are strafed by a helicopter, in a wild chase from boat to boat, through streets, houses, open-air markets and over rooftops. At her base of operations, ingeniously disguised as an innocent-looking bicycle repair shop, Wai Lin and 007 deduce the location of the craft which Carver has used to sink HMS *Devonshire*. It is a 'stealth'

ABOVE: *(left & right) Love and let die: 007's rekindled love affair with Paris Carver (Teri Hatcher)*
is cut tragically short when he returns to his hotel room to find she has been murdered.
INSET: *Teri Hatcher fan sites on the Internet number over 7,000.*

boat, completely invisible to radar and built with the help of General Chang, who had, as Wai Lin discovered a year earlier, stolen material essential for its construction. Before they leave, 007 and Wai Lin send a warning message to Beijing via computer, and leave for Ha Long Bay.

In their Zodiac dinghy, Bond and Wai Lin cruise into the cove, where they discover the state-of-the-art 'stealth' boat with its smooth planed surfaces and an utterly black finish. On board, Carver and Gupta prepare to instigate an unprovoked attack. 007 and Wai Lin board the craft and begin planting limpet mines, when Carver picks her up on the security video monitors. Stamper grabs Wai Lin and Bond goes after her. The 'stealth' boat moves into position between the British and Chinese fleets and fires a small missile at the flagship of each fleet. The ships zigzag at high speed to avoid the missiles, which explode in the water just beyond. In response, the Chinese scramble a squadron of MiGs, while on board the British flagship HMS *Bedford*, Admiral Kelly orders the launch of a harpoon missile as a warning shot. Carver orders Stamper to bring Wai Lin to him on the bridge. While removing the limpet mines hidden by the two secret agents, Stamper shoots a guard dressed by 007 in his own clothes. Believing he has killed Bond, Stamper returns to the bridge. Carver explains to Wai Lin that there are only nine short minutes before the Chinese MiGs will attack the British fleet, and then he will fire the cruise missile he has stolen from the wreck of the *Devonshire*. 007 quickly makes a simple explosive device and primes it with a detonator from his watch, and then wedges the device between two heat exchangers. With 'Air Threat Warning Red' on board HMS *Bedford*, Bond has little time to put his back-up plan into effect. 007 makes his way into Gupta's control room. Holding the man at gunpoint, he overhears Carver lecturing Wai Lin over the intercom.

Meanwhile back in England, M, without ceremony, bursts into the MOD Situation Room to inform the Minister of Defence that she's just confirmed a message from 007 via her opposite number in Beijing. Their ships should look for a boat invisible to radar. The Chinese are not the enemy; Carver has been playing both sides for fools.

Carver's intention has been that the Chinese leaders will be killed and General Chang will take over the government, negotiate a truce, and give him exclusive broadcasting rights in China for the next 50 years. Believing that Carver needs Gupta to launch the cruise missile, 007 attempts to exchange him for Wai Lin. When Gupta tells Carver the missile is ready for launch, he seals his own fate. Gesturing to Stamper for a weapon, Carver shoots Gupta dead. Simultaneously Bond activates his back-up plan: he presses the sweep button on his watch and the upper stern platform wall of the launch bay explodes with shattering force. 007 grabs Wai Lin as Carver is blown backwards by the blast, which has breached the hull, enabling the fleets to see the 'stealth' boat on radar.

ABOVE: *Paris Carver (Teri Hatcher) is classy, sophisticated and sexy: three attributes that no one would argue with concerning this lady.*

Bond and Wai Lin take on the media mogul and his crew to the death – in which 007 teaches Carver and Stamper a new definition of 'dead in the water'.

IN KEEPING with the independent, self-assured, sexually confident woman of today, the main heroine of *Tomorrow Never Dies*, Colonel Wai Lin, as portrayed by Michelle Yeoh, is a perfect reflection of the modern woman, and is a formidable ally for secret agent 007, certainly matching him talent for talent.

Michelle was born Yeoh Choo Kheng in Ipoh, Malaysia. While in high school she was active in sports, and represented Malaysia in squash, diving and swimming competitions. Her passion for ballet led her to enrol in the Royal Academy of Dance in London, where she attained an Advanced Level degree. She also received a B.A. in Creative Arts. But her ballet career was cut short by an injury. In 1983 she returned to Malaysia and entered a beauty pageant. She was crowned Miss Malaysia, as well as 'Miss Mooba' in Melbourne the same year.

In 1984 she was invited to Hong Kong to make a commercial with Jackie Chan. Instantly, she became the most sought-after new talent in the movie industry. She signed with D&B Films and made her debut in 1985 in a non-action role in the action comedy *Owls vs. Dumbo*. It was her second film, *Yes, Madam*, which established her as the premiere female action star in Asia. Her next two pictures, *Royal Warriors* (also known as *In the Line of Duty*) and *Magnificent Warriors*, further fortified her position. Her training in dance contributed to one of the unique characteristics of her acting talent – she performed her own stunts! In 1988, after only one more picture, *Easy Money*, she married and retired from the screen.

Her marriage lasted four years. Then she made an astonishing comeback. *Police Story III: Supercop*, co-starring Jackie Chan, was the top-grossing film in Asia in 1992 and Michelle became the most popular and the highest-paid actress in Asia. Typical of her stunt work is a high speed motorcycle jump on to the roof of a fast-moving train in *Supercop*. In the next two years she made a total of eight pictures, including cult classics *The Heroic Trio* and *Tai-chi Master*.

In 1995 she decided to expand her acting scope and starred in two dramatic films in a row: the period epic *The Soong Sisters* and *The Story of Ah Gum*.

In addition to her film activities, Michelle is also a committee member of the Hong Kong Cancer Fund and Honorary Patron of KELY Support Group.

Every James Bond movie has its 'sacrificial lamb', and *Tomorrow Never Dies* is no exception. Played with style and aplomb by American actress Teri Hatcher, Paris Carver is an ex-lover of James Bond who falls foul of her mad media mogul

ABOVE: *Even before her appearance in* Tomorrow Never Dies, *Michelle Yeoh was the most popular and highest-paid actress in Asia.*

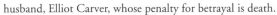

husband, Elliot Carver, whose penalty for betrayal is death.

Teri has emerged as one of the most sought-after talents on both the large and small screens. Towards the end of 1996 she earned widespread praise as part of the ensemble cast of the critically acclaimed MGM release *2 Days in the Valley*. Her other film credits include a provocative role in the erotic thriller *Heaven's Prisoners*, with Alec Baldwin and Eric Roberts. She also appeared opposite David Schwimmer in his directorial debut film *You've Been Gone*. She made her feature film debut in the Hollywood satire *The Big Picture*, starring Kevin Bacon, and her earlier work also includes a memorable part in the comedy *Soapdish*, starring Sally Field and Kevin Kline.

She is probably best known for her role as the savvy and sophisticated Lois Lane in the ABC TV series *Lois & Clark: The New Adventures of Superman*, an international hit shown in more than 35 countries. She has a huge following in the United States, and her fan sites on the Internet number over 7,000.

ABOVE: *(top) Bond and Wai Lin take the 'easy' way down from Carver's Saigon news headquarters.*
(bottom left) Wai Lin may be physically small, but she packs a kick like a mare.
(bottom right) Faced with overwhelming odds, Wai Lin keeps her cool and eliminates the enemy.

Bonds Have More Fun!

ABOVE: *(top) Sean Connery poses on the volcano set at Pinewood Studios with his female co-stars for* You Only Live Twice *(1967).*
(middle) The biggest Bond of all! Sean Connery may well look pleased with himself in this kind of company, his female co-stars in Thunderball *(1965).*
(bottom left) For On Her Majesty's Secret Service *(1969), George Lazenby slipped into the role like it was second nature, with a bevy of beauties*
including Carol Dilworth, Anita Richardson, Erika Bergman and Shakira – the future Mrs Michael Caine.
(bottom right) Roger Moore discovers that the desert does indeed hold a mysterious beauty – or four, in The Spy Who Loved Me *(1977).*

ABOVE: *(top left) Britt Ekland and Maud Adams – the Swedes who loved him, in Roger Moore's 1974 Bond thriller* The Man With The Golden Gun.
(top right) Sean Connery seems to have eyes only for Ursula Andress, regardless of the attractive distraction of Eunice Gayson and Zena Marshall in
Dr No *(1962).*
(bottom) Girls seemed to ooze from the woodwork in Roger Moore's 1979 Bond epic Moonraker.

Bonds Have More Fun!

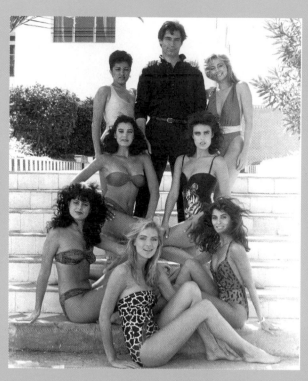

ABOVE: (top) Roger Moore was beset by blondes in the shape of Mary Stavin (left) and Carole Ashby in A View To A Kill (1985).
(left) Pierce Brosnan was partnered by two raven-haired beauties, Teri Hatcher and Michelle Yeoh for Tomorrow Never Dies (1997).
(right) Famke Janssen, Pierce Brosnan and Izabella Scorupco. It's 1995, and Bond still has women at his feet in GoldenEye.
OPPOSITE: (top left) Timothy Dalton is joined on location in Mexico by Talisa Soto (left) and Carey Lowell.
(top right) Timothy Dalton is flanked by the Bond Girls who can only be described as 'set dressing' for The Living Daylights (1987).
(bottom left) Roger Moore relaxes with some more 'set dressing' for For Your Eyes Only (1981).

The World Is Not Enough (1999)

JAMES BOND	PIERCE BROSNAN
ELEKTRA KING	SOPHIE MARCEAU
RENARD	ROBERT CARLYLE
CHRISTMAS JONES	DENISE RICHARDS
VALENTIN ZUKOVSKY	ROBBIE COLTRANE
M	JUDI DENCH
Q	DESMOND LLEWELYN
R	JOHN CLEESE
MONEYPENNY	SAMANTHA BOND
SIR ROBERT KING	DAVID CALDER
TANNER	MICHAEL KITCHEN
ROBINSON	COLIN SALMON
DOCTOR WARMFLASH	SERENA SCOTT-THOMAS
GABOR	JOHN SERU
COLONEL AKAKIEVICH	CLAUDE-OLIVER RUDOLPH
DAVIDOV	ULRICH THOMSEN
BULL	GOLDIE
CIGAR GIRL	MARIA GRAZIA CUCINOTTA
LACHAISE	PATRICK MALAHIDE
PRODUCERS	MICHAEL G. WILSON
	BARBARA BROCCOLI
DIRECTOR	MICHAEL APTED
SCREENPLAY	NEAL PURVIS AND ROBERT WADE
PRODUCTION DESIGNER	PETER LAMONT
DIRECTOR OF PHOTOGRAPHY	ADRIAN BIDDLE

JAMES BOND faces the deadliest duo of his career when an international terrorist and a power-mad heiress join forces to monopolize the world's oil market by creating a nuclear catastrophe in the Bosporus Strait.

Agent 007, having successfully collected a suitcase containing £5 million belonging to Sir Robert King from a recently assassinated contact in Bilbao, returns to MI6's Thames-side HQ with the oil industrialist's cash.

Bond meets King in M's office and is surprised by the closeness of their friendship. M and King read law at Oxford together, and she has known his daughter, Elektra, since birth. King leaves M's office to collect his cash from the 'secure room'. During his debriefing with M, Bond realizes something is wrong. A massive explosion rocks the building. King is killed instantly by the blast. Investigating the devastation, 007 is fired upon from the river. It's the Cigar Girl, whom Bond encountered in Bilbao and who was responsible for cutting off his contact with a throwing knife. Bond grabs Q's prototype jet boat and roars after her. Eventually forced to attempt a getaway in a hot-air balloon, with 007 hanging underneath on one of the anchor ropes and three military gunships closing in, she realizes escape is futile – and surrender isn't an option. The balloon explodes in a massive fireball, taking the Cigar Girl with it – but not before Bond has dropped to the relative safety of the Millennium Dome roof, injuring his shoulder. The Dome proves to be of some use after all!

Attending Sir Robert King's funeral on his Scottish estate with other high-ranking MI6 personnel, Bond gets his first sight of Elektra, who greets M, embracing her with great affection.

Afterwards at Castle Thane, the MI6 Remote Operations Centre in the Scottish Highlands, M's Deputy, Bill Tanner, debriefs Bond and other agents, explaining that the money was a highly compacted fertilizer bomb. In one of the notes the metal anti-counterfeiting strip had been replaced with magnesium, which acted as the detonator. King's lapel-pin had been switched for a copy that contained a radio-transmitter to trigger the blast. M insists that Bond should be off the active-duty list until the medical department clears him. But 007 persuades the highly attractive Dr Molly Warmflash, as only he can, to clear him for duty.

Bond tackles M about the recent kidnapping of Elektra King and discovers some unpleasant truths – and that the cash for which he had acted as courier was literally a King's ransom: the money had been intended to pay off King's daughter's kidnapper, the terrorist Renard. Instead of delivering the ransom, M sent 009 to kill Renard, but before he completed the mission, Elektra escaped. Dr Warmflash explains to M and Bond that the bullet in Renard's brain is moving through the medulla oblongata, killing off his senses. Because he feels no pain, he can push himself harder, longer than any normal man.

M sends 007 to the Caucasus Mountains to protect Elektra and discover who switched the lapel-pin, causing the

ABOVE: 'Who are you?' asks Christmas (Denise Richards). Hasn't she ever heard of Bond, James Bond?

death of her old friend. If Bond's instincts are correct, Renard will be back – and Elektra will be his next target.

Arriving at the King organization's oil pipeline, Bond introduces himself to Elektra. Trying to assess 007, Elektra probes with a personal question: 'Tell me, have you ever lost a loved one, Mr Bond?' 'I've had to give up loved ones,' replies Bond delicately. He explains that M has sent him to protect her. But she is having none of it: 'I'm trying to build an 800-mile pipeline. The Russians have three competing pipelines. They'll do anything to stop me. My father was murdered, the villagers are rioting, and you, Mr Bond, think I might be in danger? I am going to finish building this pipeline, Mr Bond – and I don't need your "help".'

Never taking no for an answer, Bond is invited to go skiing by Elektra. Suddenly they are attacked by four heavily armed parahawks – low-flying, sleek, deadly snow vehicles. Although Bond outwits his enemies and despatches them with explosive results, he and Elektra are buried alive by an avalanche caused by the destruction of the parahawks.

Bond takes Elektra back to her villa overlooking the Caspian Sea, where she explains that after the kidnapping she

ABOVE: *Christmas (Denise Richards) is indeed in deep water,*
inside a submarine which is sinking to the ocean floor.
TOP: *One more notch and Elektra (Sophie Marceau) will achieve what no other mentally deranged villain*
has succeeded in doing in over 30 years – kill James Bond.

was afraid to go outside, afraid to be alone, afraid to be in a crowd, afraid to do anything at all. She wants Bond to stay with her. He can't. She's getting too close.

Bond travels to the Casino l'Or Noir in Baku to glean information from its owner, the one man who has all the answers – his old 'friend' Valentin Zukovsky. At the casino legitimate businessmen rub shoulders with the scum of the earth. Bond is irritated by the arrival of Elektra in such a place; even though her bodyguard, Gabor, accompanies her, it hardly makes 007's protection duties any easier. Zukovsky extends Elektra the courtesy of her late father's credit line of $1 million. 'You're determined to protect me, aren't you?' she exclaims. 'There's no point in living if you can't feel alive,' she tells Bond, and promptly loses the million to Zukovsky in a high-stakes game of blackjack. Bond senses their shared need for risk; he's falling for this woman in a big way. After returning to her villa, they spend a long, languorous night making love.

Leaving Elektra sleeping, Bond investigates a nearby office and discovers Davidov, King's head of security, attempting to hide the corpse of Dr Arkov, a scientist from the Russian Atomic Energy department, whose identity he has taken. Bond is forced to kill Davidov and assume Arkov's identity himself.

Catching the Russian transport plane meant for Arkov, 007 lands at the nuclear test facility in Kazakhstan, where scientists from the International Decommissioning Agency are safely disposing of corroding hydrogen bombs. A Colonel Akakievich introduces Bond to the IDA physicist in charge of the project: Dr Christmas Jones, an American in her mid-twenties. As she removes her protective suit, Bond can see why

ABOVE: (top left) 007 (Pierce Brosnan) falls for Elektra (Sophie Marceau) in a big way, a feeling he is to regret bitterly. (top right) Christmas Jones (Denise Richards) and secret agent James Bond escape from a nuclear test chamber in the nick of time.

her Russian colleagues can hardly take their eyes off her. Dressed in a revealing tank top and shorts – and sporting an incongruous Peace tattoo around her navel – Dr Jones leaves an indelible impression.

In the heart of the nuclear test chamber Bond takes Renard by surprise, holding him at gunpoint. Renard explains that if he doesn't make a telephone call in 20 minutes, Elektra will die. Bond believes he is bluffing. Renard antagonizes him: 'Beautiful, isn't she? You should have had her before. When she was innocent. Before she was such a whore in bed. How does it feel? To know I broke her in for you?' Furious, Bond strikes him across the temple with his pistol. Renard drops to his knees. 'A man tires of being executed,' he sighs. 'But then again, there's no point in living if you can't feel alive.' Just about to squeeze the trigger, Bond freezes at this statement. He's lost his chance. Into the test chamber walk Dr Jones, two armed soldiers and Colonel Akakievich, who orders Bond to drop his gun. Christmas has discovered that Bond is an impostor – Dr Arkov was 63 years old. Bond is unable to convince the colonel that Renard and his men are impostors and are in the process of stealing a nuclear bomb. Throwing his

gun to the floor, he is grabbed by Renard, who deliberately jabs his hand into 007's injured shoulder. Bond's mind races. How did Renard know about his injury?

Renard and his men open fire, killing the colonel and his men. Bond and Christmas escape from the test chamber in the nick of time with the aid of 007's special Omega watch – but Renard and his men have also escaped with the bomb after removing its locator card so that it's impossible to track.

Back at Castle Thane, M takes a call on the video line from Elektra in Baku, who explains that her head of security has been found murdered and Bond has disappeared. Meanwhile Bond finds his way back to Elektra's villa, where, after dealing with Gabor, he accuses her of being in league with Renard. 'After all, "there's no point in living if you can't feel alive". Isn't that right, Elektra?' She denies she knows what 007 is talking about. 'I think you do. It's called Stockholm Syndrome,' he retorts. 'A young impressionable victim. Sheltered, sexually inexperienced. A powerful kidnapper skilled in torture, in manipulation. Something snaps in the victim's mind. The captive falls in love with her captor.' Time for psychoanalysis is cut short when Elektra receives a telephone call informing her that Renard is back and five men have been killed at the pipeline control centre. Bond and Elektra leave immediately.

The MI6 military helicopter carrying M lands at the murder site in Turkey. M takes Bond to one side; she wants an

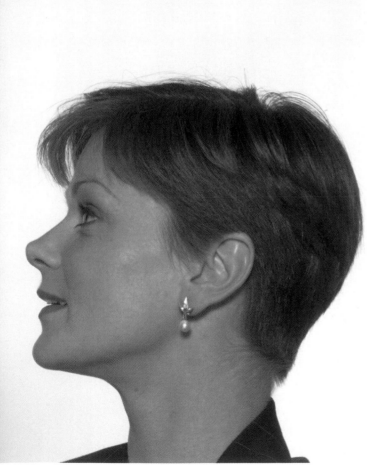

ABOVE: (left) 'What would I do without you?' Bond is forever attracted to Moneypenny (Samantha Bond). (right) Close but no cigar! Maria Grazia Cucinotta fails to dislodge 007 from the anchor ropes hanging underneath the baloon in which she is trying to escape.

update. Giving M the bomb's locator card, 007 is unable to convince her that Elektra is 'the inside woman' who switched her father's lapel-pin. Christmas reports that her team can find no sign of the bomb. Bond realizes that Renard has placed it in the pipeline on an observation rig heading for the oil terminal. 'Now do you believe me?' Elektra asks Bond, who thinks Renard is going for the oil. Bond, quick-witted as ever, races by helicopter with Christmas to an access hatch ahead of the bomb-laden rig, where together they ride another rig in a hair-raising attempt to defuse the bomb, watched anxiously by M and Elektra on the pipeline map. The rig carrying the bomb explodes.

Back at the pipeline control centre, M is crestfallen, believing Bond and Dr Jones have been killed. Elektra offers her condolences with crocodile tears and a surprise gift for M – her father's original lapel-pin. M looks at Elektra, horrified, as Gabor shoots M's bodyguards. M gives Elektra a blood-curdling glare as the girl explains, 'I was terribly upset when the money didn't kill both of you. Then you dropped the answer right in my lap: Bond. As you say, he's the best you have. Or should I say, "had"?' M gives Elektra a stinging blow to the face before being restrained by her guards.

Back at the ruptured pipeline Bond tells Christmas why he let the bomb explode: 'She thinks we're dead. And she thinks she got away with it.' Bond explains that Elektra has blown up her own pipeline to make herself look even more innocent. Robinson replies to 007's radio call: 'Red Alert: M is missing with Elektra. Three men down. Await instructions.' Bond believes he may have overlooked one critical element. 'What? More plutonium?' asks Christmas. 'No,' replies Bond. 'Beluga.'

During the twilight hours a boat puts in at the Maiden's Tower, an ancient edifice in the middle of the Bosporus. Renard disembarks with several of his retinue. Elektra greets him with open arms before taking him to view the incarcerated M. 'I hope you're proud of what you did to her,' protests M. Renard isn't impressed: 'I'm afraid you're the one who deserves credit. When I took her she was promise itself. And you left her at the mercy of a man like me. You ruined her. For what? To get to me? She's worth fifty of me!' Before leaving, Renard places a small travel clock on a stool just out of M's reach through her cell bars. 'Watch these hands, M. At noon tomorrow, your time is up. You will die along with everyone in this city and the bright, starry, oil-driven future of the West.'

ABOVE: *Perverse partners! Renard (Robert Carlyle) and Elektra (Sophie Marceau) rekindle their fascination for each other, formed between kidnapper and victim.*

Bond and Christmas pay a visit to Zukovsky at his caviare factory in the City of Walkways, an amazing network of raised walkways and platforms built over a natural harbour, extending as far as the eye can see. Learning Bond is still alive, Elektra unsuccessfully attempts to wipe out her foes at the caviare factory with helicopters carrying giant rotating saws. Bond eventually 'persuades' Zukovsky to explain that Elektra was paying him off at his casino for certain Russian machinery he is having smuggled to her by his nephew Nikoli, a captain in the Russian navy. When Zukovsky inadvertently mentions the old days when they had hundreds of places where a submarine could surface undetected, Bond realizes the enormity of Renard and Elektra's plan: 'He's not interested in the cargo. They want the sub.' Christmas agrees: 'That's it! Put weapons-grade plutonium in that sub's reactor: instant catastrophic meltdown.' The explosion will destroy the whole of Istanbul and contaminate the Bosporus for decades. There'd be only one way to get the oil out, through the south, the King pipeline – Elektra's pipeline.

M remembers she has the bomb locator card in her pocket. All she needs to do is get her hands on the batteries inside the clock outside her cell. She could then activate a GPS tracking signal by which she can be located. But when she attempts to pull the stool towards her, it catches on the uneven stone floor and the clock tumbles well out of her reach.

The Russian submarine arrives in the tower's secret quay and Renard greets Nikoli and his skeleton crew with brandy and food.

As Gabor takes a bowl of gruel to M, Elektra appears in the doorway. She has come to gloat. Seeing the clock near her feet, Elektra picks it up and hands it to M through the bars: 'Time for you to die!' Clutching the clock, M returns to her bed.

Still with Zukovsky's radio operator, Christmas recognizes a GPS signal. Bond realizes it's the locator card. The refreshments offered to Nikoli and his submarine crew were poisoned. Surveying the grisly scene, Renard orders his men to dispose of their bodies in the sea. As they drag Nikoli away his hat falls to the ground. Renard picks it up and puts it on.

ABOVE: *(left) Dr Molly Warmflash (Serena Scott-Thomas) gives 007 a clean bill of health, noting –*
he has exceptional stamina!
(right) Red hot and dangerous! Elektra King isn't the kind of woman you'd take home to mother.

Captured by Gabor and his henchmen, Bond and Christmas are incarcerated in the Maiden's Tower. The reactor is secured. Elektra's helicopter will be collecting her in half an hour. Renard knows this is the end of the affair. 'No. It is the beginning,' says Elektra. Renard lays down Nikoli's hat and tries to mask his sorrow. He reaches to touch Elektra's cheek, but stops himself: 'The future is yours. Have fun with it.' He hands her the hat and returns to the sub.

Elektra has Christmas taken to Renard, while she leads Bond to a silk-covered chair and makes him sit. Bond and Christmas exchange a look as Gabor takes her away. 'Pretty thing. You had her too?' says Elektra. Bond ignores her. 'I could have given you the world,' she says. But Bond is unimpressed. 'The world is not enough.' 'Foolish sentiment,' replies Elektra. 'Family motto,' counters Bond. Ignoring 007's comment, Elektra casually reaches behind his neck and flips up a wooden arm to which is attached a metal collar. Bond recoils as she fastens the garrotte. 'Five more turns and your neck will break.' Elektra is enjoying herself. Since she was a child she has always had power over men, a power which she intends to use

ABOVE: *(left) Beware of buxom dark strangers bearing gifts! In this case, the Cigar Girl (Maria Grazia Cucinotta). (right) Sophie Marceau and Pierce Brosnan take a break on BMW's finest during the filming of* The World Is Not Enough.

to its full advantage in the future. She continues to rant: 'When I realized my father wouldn't rescue me from the kidnappers, I knew I had to form a new alliance. He killed me the day he refused to pay my ransom.' Bond plays for time as he works feverishly at his bound wrists. 'Was this all about oil?' he asks. 'It is my oil! Mine and my family's!' storms Elektra. 'It runs in my veins, thicker than blood. I'm going to redraw the map. And when I am through, the whole world will know my name, my grandfather's name, the glory of my people.' She straddles Bond in the chair, turning the screw several more notches. 'You should have killed me when you had the chance. But you couldn't. Not me. A woman you've loved.' She is about to turn the screw to the last notch when she is distracted by gunshots outside. Big, battered and bloody, Zukovsky is leaving a boat, moving over the rocks with three of his men.

Inside the room Elektra moves towards her gun. The doors burst open. Zukovsky walks in. The enraged giant eyes Bond in the chair. His gaze falls on the hat that Renard had brought up from below. He knows at once what it means. 'Bring it to me,' he orders Elektra. She picks it up and walks to him, surreptitiously sliding her gun beneath it. As she proffers the hat, she shoots the big Russian three times. He falls to the ground, mortally wounded, but dredges up a final ounce of energy to raise his walking-stick off the ground, which fires a shot at Bond. The bullet hits the binding at 007's wrist and splinters the wood. Zukovsky's head slumps and he stares at Bond. Comrades in arms. Then the light fades from Zukovsky's eyes. Elektra has missed the point entirely, believing that the Russian hated Bond enough to kill him in his final moments.

As Elektra leans towards Bond to administer the killer twist, 007's hand breaks free and grabs her throat. He hurls her backwards and the gun flies from her grasp. As he goes for her gun, the body of one of Zukovsky's men crashes through the window, followed by Gabor, who fires wildly at Bond with a machine-gun. Bond coolly puts him away with two quick shots. He turns back to see Elektra disappearing up the spiral staircase, and races up after her, clutching Zukovsky's dropped gun. On the way up the staircase he suddenly swings to his right at an unexpected but familiar voice: 'Bond.' 007 kicks open the door, blasts the lock off M's cell door and frees her. He turns to go upwards, after Elektra. 'Go after the submarine, forget the girl. Bond!' shouts M. 007 corners Elektra and orders her to call off Renard with a walkie-talkie. Elektra's face breaks into a perverted grin: 'You wouldn't kill me. You'd miss me.' She shouts into the walkie-talkie to Renard: 'Dive! Bond...' 007 shoots her. 'I never miss,' he says coldly, staring at her dead body for a second. Crouching, he touches her cheek once before leaving. Behind him, unnoticed, M has witnessed it all. From the balcony, Bond dives to the sea below and surfaces close to the exiting submarine, which is preparing to dive.

Once on board, 007 works his way through Renard's crew until he locates the cabin in which Christmas is

imprisoned. Holding what's left of the crew at gunpoint, he is surprised by Renard when the terrorist returns to the reactor room and orders his men to shoot 007. Everyone dives for cover as Bond and Renard exchange fire. The gun battle rages until the buoyancy controls are hit, causing the sub to tilt further and further until it hangs vertically in the water.

With the rest of the crew crushed by falling chairs and desks, Bond and Christmas are left with only one man to contend with – Renard. Trapped in the overheating reactor room, Bond and Renard are locked in a vicious fight. Renard backhands Christmas, knocking her over the railing. As Renard forces the plutonium rod deeper into the reactor, Bond wraps a piece of cloth around his hand, grabs an uncoupled steam hose

ABOVE: *The most beautiful nuclear physicist in the world – Dr Christmas Jones (Denise Richards).*

and attaches it to the reactor. Suddenly the built-up pressure of the steam blows out the rod, which pierces Renard through the heart. Renard stares at Bond in horror as he falls past Christmas. Bond and Christmas escape from the sunken submarine in its mine-launching tubes. Below them the submarine explodes in spectacular fashion.

At night on a magnificent rooftop garden looking out over Istanbul, Bond and Christmas are alone, sharing a bottle of Bollinger Grande Année 1990. Fireworks explode. They clink their glasses and Bond looks out over the city: 'I've always wanted to have Christmas in Turkey.' 'Was that a Christmas joke?' asks Dr Jones. 'From me?' says Bond. 'Never.'

THE WOMEN'S roles in the nineteenth James Bond film, *The World Is Not Enough*, are probably the strongest written of any in the series and reflect the changing attitudes towards the female sex as the twenty-first century dawns.

Elektra King, as portrayed by brown-eyed French actress Sophie Marceau, is all things to all men: beautiful, strong, vulnerable, sexy, erotic, the antagonist but also the victim. Born Sophie Maupu in Paris on 17 November 1966, she began acting in films at 14. She learned from a friend that director Claude Pinoteau was looking for new faces for a teen movie called *La Boum*. The film was very well received and became a huge success in France. This led to a sequel in 1982, not unnaturally titled *La Boum 2*, for which Sophie received the 1983 Caesar for Most Promising Actress. She has since become one of the most popular and respected actresses in her own country. Though she is still not an international star, her leading role in *The World Is Not Enough* could set the record straight. Her first English-speaking role was in Mel Gibson's Oscar-winning *Braveheart*, in which she portrayed William Wallace's love interest, Princess Isabelle. In 1995 she directed her first film, *L'Aube à l'envers*, an eight-minute short based on a screenplay she wrote while filming *Braveheart*. The film was well received at Cannes the following year. On 24 July 1995 Sophie gave birth to her first child, Vincent. She is an outspoken opponent of blood sports, and in addition to her work for animal welfare is a patron of Arc-en-Ciel ('Rainbow'), an organization which helps sick children realize their dreams.

Nuclear physicists don't come any more attractive than American actress Denise Richards. And when they're also named Christmas Jones, you know you're talking James Bond girl. Born in Downers Grove, Illinois, on 17 February 1972, Denise later moved to California, and went on to graduate from El Camino High School in Oceanside in 1989. After high school she started modelling in Paris, Tokyo and New York. Soon she got her first TV role, in *Life Goes On*, which helped her to land more TV walk-on roles and parts in movies. Her real break came with a starring role in Paul Verhoeven's *Starship Troopers*. Other roles followed, in *Wild Things* and *Drop Dead Gorgeous*. Her TV appearances include *Married With Children*, *Lois & Clark*, *Weird Science* and *Melrose Place*.

If smoking causes heart disease it's no wonder that a man's life expectancy could be cut short by 'the Cigar Girl', Renard's lethal knife-throwing partner. It isn't a trick cigar that goes bang around her – it's her high-velocity rifle as she blasts away at 007 from the back of her speedboat. Alas, we see all too little of her before she goes up, up and away in an explosive balloon. Born in Messina, Sicily, Maria Grazia Cucinotta started working as a model when she was 16, in Milan during her summer holidays. When she finished school she abandoned modelling because she didn't like the fact that clients used just her body, not her head. Maria auditioned in Rome for the TV programme *Indietro Tutta*, and was given the role of the odalisque. Meanwhile she took acting and elocution lessons to eradicate her Sicilian accent, and was taken on by an acting agency. However, she continued to work in television in order to earn a living. While film auditions were almost always a failure, her advertising jobs went well, and she started to shoot one commercial after another. These also proved an excellent learning ground for technique, as well as allowing her to meet international directors and become known abroad. Her first major film was Massimo Troisi's *Il Postino* (1994), which gave her international recognition. Her first American film was *Brooklyn State of Mind*, directed by Frank Rainone.

ABOVE: *A rare and special beauty – Sophie Marceau brings a touch of class to the proceedings in*
The World Is Not Enough